14 STEPS
TO HAPPINESS

14 Steps
to Happiness

A Program for Overcoming Depression

Kristian Hall

**FAKKEL
FORLAG**

Also by Kristian Hall:

Rise from Darkness

14 Steps to Happiness - Workbook

© Fakkel Forlag AS

Drøbak, Norway

First published in Norway in 2018, originally titled *Glad igjen!*

Published in English translation 2020

Translated by Christine Nicholson

ISBN: 978-82-999887-8-0

Dedicated to everyone who struggles with depression;
Know that a better life is possible!

TABLE OF CONTENTS

Preface 9

I Stand by Your Side 13

Introduction 15

A Plan for How to Get Out of Depression 25

14 STEPS OUT OF DEPRESSION 47

Step 1: Decide to Get Better – and Believe You Can 49

Step 2: Eat Yourself Happy 61

Step 3: Exercise Your Way to Happiness 69

Step 4: Find Sources of Joy 77

Step 5: Sleep Better 85

Step 6: Use Therapy Efficiently 97

Step 7: Become Radically Grateful 103

Step 8: Cultivate the Good People 111

Step 9: Identify Triggers and Domino Effects 127

Step 10: Get a Black Belt in Cognitive Techniques 135

Step 11: Create Meaning in Your Life 165

Step 12: Increase Your Sense of Achievement 171

Step 13: Learn Meditation, Mindfulness and
    Self-hypnosis 185

Step 14: Learn to Love Yourself 203

The Weekly Program 211

The Way Forward 219

Thank You 221

Appendix A: Glossary 225

Appendix B: List of Thought Fallacies 229

Appendix C: Further Reading and Resources 233

Appendix D: Sleep Log 237

Appendix E: Form for Extended ABC 241

PREFACE

The first time I met Kristian, we were our early twenties and both studying in Trondheim. He was studying engineering, while I was studying psychology. We were a part of a group leading an international student festival and we worked closely together for a period of time. It became obvious to me that Kristian struggled with something at the time, but I was not yet aware it was depression.

It is commonly accepted that it is difficult to tell if someone is struggling with depression. The term *hidden disease* is often used to describe a range of conditions, and aptly so, as most illnesses and diseases are difficult for others to detect. Still, depression is the most prevalent of the hidden diseases. So many people are affected that it is safe to say it is a global pandemic.

Being depressed is a terrible experience in itself, and to make matters worse, many people feel that they are met with little or no understanding from others in relation to their disease. Mental health issues are still, to a large degree, misunderstood and are often met with attitudes like *just pull yourself together and you will be okay*. Imagine if physical and mental illnesses were met in the same way? *Are you in bed with pneumonia again? Pull yourself together and go to work.* Or: *I have to drive Maria to school just because she broke her leg. When is she going to start taking responsibility for her own life?*

I believe that this book, in addition to helping the depressed person, will give families, relatives, and those close to the depressed a better understanding of the disease. It will discuss exactly what depression entails and what can be done to lessen the burden for the depressed and improve their quality of life.

The healthcare system often gives depression the cold shoulder. For a busy family doctor it is, sadly, often easier to reach for the prescription pad, even though official health authorities, such as the Norwegian Directorate of Health, have determined that counselling and psychological treatment should be the treatment of choice for mild and moderate depression. Self-help methods have also been proven to have a considerable positive impact on depression.

So what is depression? The official definition used in Norway is that given by the UN through WHO's ICD-10 manual. There, the signs of depression are listed as: low mood, lack of interest and joy, and lack of energy resulting in lethargy and reduced activity. Symptoms also include:

- reduced concentration and focus
- reduced self-esteem and self-confidence
- feelings of guilt and inferiority
- sad and pessimistic thoughts about the future
- contemplating self-harm or suicide
- trouble sleeping
- reduced appetite

People struggling with depression are afflicted with these symptoms to various degrees, and some of the symptoms might not be present at all.

This book is divided into different steps. Some of them are general and help fight all the symptoms; for instance, Step 1: *Decide to Get Better - and Believe You Can*, Step 2: *Eat Yourself Happy*, Step 3: *Exercise Your Way to Happiness* and Step 6: *Use Therapy Efficiently.* Other steps are more targeted at specific symptoms: Step 5: *Sleep Better,* is aimed at troubled sleep, Step 11: *Create Meaning in Your Life*, is aimed at reducing the feeling of meaninglessness, and Step 13: *Learn Mindfulness, Meditation and Self-hypnosis,* is aimed at combating stress and poor sleep.

The book is unique in its alternation between practical aids and, at times, powerful examples from the author's own struggle with depression. This makes the text relatable and helps it come to life. If you are struggling with this same affliction, it could be a great help to you to see how he used these techniques to get rid of his own depression.

In addition to the program in the book, I would recommend the following: if you are having suicidal thoughts, have been unable to go work for a while due to low mood, or constantly feel unable to cope with the demands of everyday life, seek professional help. It is of particular importance to get help if you have children in your care. The first step is to speak to your doctor.

Best of luck on your journey!

Knut-Petter Sætre Langlo
Psychologist and specialist in Neuropsychology
and Adult Psychology

I STAND BY YOUR SIDE

A few years ago, I watched a documentary about venomous spiders. One part of the documentary was about an American, who several years prior had been bitten by a black widow spider. If bitten by this spider, you have roughly 24 hours of agony ahead of you. Severe pain, dizziness, hallucinations and nausea. The effects of the venom will slowly subside over time.

The man in the film went out every single night with a flashlight and a hammer. He wanted to kill as many black widow spiders as he possibly could, as he hated them so intently after the agonizing 24 hours he had once experienced.

I have a similar relationship with depression. Depression robbed me of joy for a whole decade of my life. It was ten years of pain, resignation and frustration; a decade where my life was on hold.

I am painfully aware of how many people are, in this very moment, suffering from this disease. So, I am out with my flashlight and hammer.

One of my life's missions is to help as many people as possible get out of depression. My first book, *Rise from Darkness,* as well as this book, are parts of that mission.

A frequent comment from readers of *Rise from Darkness* is that they appreciate my own personal presence in the text and that I write about depression based on my own experiences. In this book, I am taking it one step further. In the introduction I have included snippets from my personal diaries from when my depression was at its worst, as well as when I was on my way to recovery. These snippets are unedited, with swearwords, typos, warts and all. I think it will be useful for you to read them so you can follow my development, and most importantly, see that it IS possible to recover from depression.

I have gone from wanting to die every day to really loving my life. I still have difficulties in my life (as we all do), but I am now able to put myself in the driver's seat and my problems in the back seat, focus on the wonderful world we live in and all the fantastic people in it.

What I want is for you to follow me and leave the dark struggles of depression behind. Although I have never met you, I sincerely wish that you will get better and improve your quality of life. I stand by your side.

Kristian Hall

Introduction

Depression is an awful illness that can remove all joy of living, paralyze you, and put your life on hold. It can rob you of sleep, energy, friends, hope and opportunities. Depression comes in many different forms which all manifest differently, but the typical depressed person can be described like this:

You see yourself as a clown, a parasite feeding off other peoples' lives and happiness, a burden, someone who should simply disappear. You feel guilty for so many things, for receiving social benefits, or for the pain you are putting your family through. You believe no one loves you, and that no one ever will. You feel like you have never accomplished anything and that you likely never will. Everything is hopeless. You have no energy or motivation to improve your situation. You are constantly tired, even though you spend 12 hours or more every day in bed. You cannot stand spending time with others as you do not think you have anything to contribute and you do not wish to inconvenience others with your presence.

You feel that no one understands you, and to a certain degree, you are right. Being depressed is like being from a different planet. You see yourself, your surroundings and the world through dark sunglasses. Many people will tell you that you just have to pull yourself together, but you are not able to. Since you believe you are unable to succeed at anything, the depression will gradually get worse.

This will continue until you turn the process around and understand that what has caused the dark eclipse in your mind and your thought processes can, in fact, disappear. This is what I will help you with.

A global study from 2018, referred to by the WHO, estimates that more than 264 million people worldwide suffer from depression. It is estimated that 16.2 million adults in the United States, or 6.7 percent of American adults, suffer from depression in any given year. That means that most of us knows at least one person who suffers from depression. WHO lists depression as one of the world's most costly illnesses. Depression is a potentially deadly illness. In 2017 there were 47,173 recorded suicides in the US, according to the Centre for Disease Control and Prevention (CDC). Not everyone who takes their own life suffers from depression, but according to the CDC, more than half suffer from serious depression. Unfortunately, some people give up when life seems completely hopeless.

However, you *can* recover from depression! I am living proof of that. If complete recovery seems too ambitious a goal for you, you can at the very least aim to make a big improvement. All it takes is systematic work over time along two dimensions. The first dimension is *what you do*. The second is *how you think*.

You might think that this sounds too easy. No wonder, as one of the major elements of depression is that you are robbed of the belief that it is possible to get better. I will do my best to help you regain that belief.

As a reader of this book, you may not suffer from depression yourself, but rather have a family member or friend who does.

Sometimes, being the next of kin or a friend to someone with depression can be worse than suffering from the illness yourself, as you are powerless to change how a person experiences life. There are many things you can do to help, but in the end, the afflicted person will need to do the work him or herself.

The way you as a family member or a friend can help is to gain knowledge about what depression is. This way, you will be better equipped to understand the depressed person. Then you can cheer them on from the sidelines and help motivate them when they need an extra push. You can suggest techniques and different measures for the depressed person to start practicing. Thereafter, you can initiate activities you know will make the depressed person happier – preferably something you can do together.

Let me illustrate the starting point for my own road out of depression, with a rather glum journal excerpt from one of my most painful years:

> *Resignation. Worse than Depression. I feel like I'm sitting still in a loose railcar that is slowly but surely moving toward the edge of a cliff. It's not the usual irrational depression that is tearing me down now. It's unfortunately something much worse. It's my own conclusion, after having carefully analyzed my life using logic and reason. My life is not bearable. No matter what scenario I picture, the conclusion is that the best and quickest way out is to hang myself. I feel nothing except loneliness and resignation. The lift is on its way toward the end and I don't give a shit.*
>
> *Two things make this situation fucked up. First of all, the fact that I can never take my own life. If I could, everything would really be quite simple. Then I could live one day at a*

time, and once things got too difficult, I could simply end it all. The second matter complicating the situation is my never-ending longing for love and intimacy.
I cannot see a solution.

This excerpt shows how dark it can get in the mind of a depressed person. I got out of the darkness and gradually got to a point where I now love my life, using the very same techniques and measures you will read about in this book. Like everyone else, I have good days and bad days, worries and grief, but overall, I am now able to focus on all the beautiful and fantastic things life has to offer. They are available in your life too; you just cannot see them yet.

Here is the catch: A person lacking confidence, hope, drive, energy and dreams for the future, is somehow to get rid of his/ her poor thinking and emotional response patterns that cause the depression. How on earth is this possible?

In 1977, a British man, George Meegan, started what still stands as the longest uninterrupted walk in the world. He walked over 30,000 km (19,000 miles) and crossed South and North America, from the southernmost point in Chile, to the northernmost point in Alaska. It took him over six years and he walked an average of 12 km (7.5 miles) per day.

The same method can be used to fight depression. You take the first step, even if it's only a small one. Then you take another one. You then continue until you notice things are starting to take on a rhythm of their own and becoming automatic. I promise you it will gradually become easier.

One keyword here is patience. Depression can take years to develop and it can take months, even years, before you see a real improvement, although you will notice an increasing sense of achievement and joy during the process. But the hard work will be worth it. The reward is enormous; it is about your whole life, about all the days to come from this moment on. Although you can expect it to be tough, there will also be times when you will feel hopeful and optimistic, when your energy and motivation returns – this because you can see that you are moving forward!

This book includes 14 steps on how to get out of depression. You will start with the simplest steps when you are at your worst. The measures I suggest then will gradually increase in complexity.

It is fully possible to get rid of depression and, at the very least, to live a much, much improved life. My story is an example of exactly that.

MY STORY

I was born in Oslo, Norway, on August 11,1977. In 1973, my mother met the man who would turn out to be the love of her life: my dad. My dad was intelligent and very creative. At times he ran four to five businesses simultaneously and several of them turned good profits. He was artistic and I still have some of his paintings hanging on my wall. Dad was one of the kindest people I have ever known, with a kindness that was sometimes exploited by others. His kindness also made him very loved. His funeral was held at Vestre Aker Chapel, one of the largest chapels in Oslo, and there were so many people attending that there was not enough room for them all.

Sadly, Dad also had a dark side. My guess is that if he had lived today he would have been diagnosed with bipolar disorder. He showed all the symptoms: manic periods of gambling and crazy ideas, as well as strong anxiety and deep depression. He abused alcohol and medication. My sister and I never knew what condition he would be in when we came home from school. On several occasions during my childhood I was alone with my dad when he was so drunk that he could barely take care of himself.

He burned the candle at both ends. His hard life and an underlying illness made his heart give up and stop for good on September 14, 1991. I was 14 years old.

When I look at photos of myself as a 13-year-old or younger, I see a high-spirited, happy-go-lucky, strong boy. I had a happy childhood, in spite of many frightening experiences. I would never swap my childhood, or my dad, for anything. But in later photos, taken when I was 14 or older, my smile and my spirit are gone. I was an angry teenager and I gradually lost all my friends. I don't blame them – I had become a rather unpleasant person. I was very easily insulted and blamed others for almost everything that went wrong, regardless what it was.

My grief gradually turned into depression and my mind was full of twisted thought patterns and over-critical inner voices whose judgements were torturous. After a while I lost the will to live and not a day went by where I did not fantasize about killing myself.

I reached rock bottom during my military service, which at the time was mandatory for all young men in Norway. I was a tank loader, and the combination of engine noises and machine-gun fire gave me tinnitus. It is a symphony of constant quite loud and high-pitched ringing noises in my head that I will likely have to live with for the rest of my life. Due to my hearing loss, I was taken off combat duty and put in an office, where I sat for six months with little to do but stare at the walls. It is a mystery how I got through those six months.

What kept me alive through the most difficult years was my love for my mom and my sister, Henriette. As I was well aware of how painful it is to lose a close family member, I could not put them through that again.

After my military service I began studying engineering at NTNU in Trondheim. By then, I had managed to improve my social situation, and had built up a social network of friends that I really enjoyed spending time with. This was a crucial step in rebuilding myself.

Ever since Dad had died, Mom and Henriette had tried to get me to get help. Grief-groups at first, and once they realized I had developed depression, they suggested therapy. I refused. I was convinced it was impossible to get help, that everything was hopeless and that nothing would ever get better.

Luckily, after years of effort, they eventually managed to persuade me. I contacted the student health services in Trondheim, who put me in touch with a psychologist. The psychologist was a very wise man and an experienced therapist. He helped me sort through my feelings, particularly in relation to my complicated grief over my dad's passing. I went to therapy, sometime twice a week, and it was hard, hard work. I remember being so dizzy and lightheaded after the sessions that I would stagger down the road.

The work paid off gradually, and after a period of intense anger toward Dad. *Why did you die and leave us behind? Why could not you handle your own problems so you could find your joy of living again?* I finally stood on emotionally firm ground. I had taken the edge off my depression. My suicidal thoughts were less intense and less frequent. My depression had gone from constant to intermittent. Here is an excerpt from my diaries from this period, where it is evident that the feeling of hopelessness had partly changed into frustration over not moving forward faster:

8 October 1999, 7:42pm

And so it happened again. I have gone from a period of relative happiness to sudden depression. What is different this time around is that I have thought a lot about how I have changed, so I am partly prepared. I have known this whole week that whenever I am happy with the status quo, sooner or later, everything will turn into hell in a handbasket. The trigger to set it all in motion could be anything. So, as I am now sitting here and things have collapsed, I know exactly the situation I find myself in. I know why things that were merely trivial yesterday knocked me even further down today. What I don't know, though, is how to turn it around. Only when I find that truth can I become a successful person. I don't really know if today can be considered a step in that direction. I truly hope so, as it's so damn difficult to live like this.

Compared with the earlier excerpt, the improvement is obvious. But I still found life hard and I was still a victim to what I call logical fallacies. Logical fallacies are adverse, automatic, and irrational thought patterns. They are described under Step 10 – Cognitive Techniques. Here is an example from another journal excerpt:

November 8, 1999, 6:59 pm

Everyone is happy. They are partying. I'm sitting in my room, listening to Portishead and feeling like shit. Pathetic. I see no solution. Regardless of what happens to me, I'll always have relapses like these. The depression controls everything, I cannot function. People notice and they look at me like I'm crazy. In a manner of speaking, that is what I am. Well, I'm not actually crazy, just different from just about everyone else, and that is fucking difficult.

This excerpt implies that if you are hurting right now, you will *always* hurt. That is not true. Life is dynamic, not static, and that goes for all of us, because our brains are constantly changing.

Although at this point in time, as a 22-year-old, I had greatly improved, I had a strong need to *completely* rid my mind of its inner demons. I started reading psychology textbooks and self-help books. I came across positive psychology and cognitive behavioral therapy (CBT). I devoured all of it. Here were all the techniques that could help me recover completely! I started applying different techniques to silence my inner hyperactive and mean critics. I taught myself radical gratitude, something that entails *grabbing hold of what is actually good in life*, even if you are drowning in negative emotions.

Gradually, I went further and further into the stage where the improvement happens automatically. The poor habits, where I would talk myself down, were replaced by a new mindset and new thinking patterns where I lifted myself up. I got more friends and even a girlfriend! In the span of a few months, my girlfriend and I moved in together. Today we are married and have a wonderful son.

In 2005, I started noting down fragments of what helped get rid of depression, based on my own experiences. Eventually, I had a large number of notes and I decided to compile them and turn them into a book. *Rise from Darkness* was published in 2015. I felt that I had realized something crucial regarding what works when fighting depression. I had, throughout the years, longed for a recipe I could follow in order to recover, but no one seemed to have one.

It is my calling to reach out to as many people as possible who are currently suffering from depression, with a simple message: *You can improve significantly, and it is easier than you think!*

As I am writing this, I have just moved to Drøbak, and I feel I am living a deeply meaningful life, surrounded by people who fill my days with joy. I have realized that the positive development that leads out of depression does not stop. You can, to a steadily increasing degree, learn to hold on to the good sides of life, and learn not to dwell on the painful aspects of life that inevitably exist for everyone. After a while it will become a habit where you think *oh well, no big deal,* when something adverse happens.

Even though the next journal excerpt is somewhat pompous, it very well describes how I am feeling right now. It is interesting to compare it with the first excerpt in the introduction.

June 27, 2015, 11:17pm

I have been knocked down a lot, but I am now living a very fulfilling life.

Despite everything, in spite of my sometimes difficult childhood, in spite of my depression, there were a lot of good things earlier too. I had Dad, who after all was 1,000 times funnier than most people. I have Mom and Henriette. I have all my friends. And I have Kirsten. And Falk.

I love Falk so much it often hurts. I understand how Henriette and I must have been huge sources of light in Dad's life.

I now know where I am going.

This change is possible for you too. All you need is to work systematically over time, using the techniques you find here.

A Plan for How to Get Out of Depression

Any complex challenge is best managed with a plan. Getting rid of depression is definitely a complex challenge. The good news is that I have already done the planning for you – this book![1]

This book contains 14 steps, all of which will help you recover or significantly improve from depression. I realize that 14 steps might sound like a lot, but they are necessary in order to attack the depression from all angles and with a holistic approach. This will make it easier for you to recover, partly because we are all different, and we all need different approaches in order to get better. There are lots of things you can do to get better, and in the program you will focus on only one step at a time.

---

[1] Self-help, like the measures and techniques you will find in this book, are meant to be a supplement to, and not a replacement for, traditional treatment of depression. Follow the advice of your doctor, psychiatrist and your therapist, at the same time as you are working with the program on your own.

AN OVERVIEW OF THE 14 STEPS OUT OF DEPRESSION

1. Decide to Get Better - and Believe You Can
2. Eat Yourself Happy
3. Exercise Your Way to Happiness
4. Find Sources of Joy
5. Sleep Better
6. Use Therapy Efficiently
7. Become Radically Grateful
8. Cultivate the Good People
9. Identify Triggers and Domino Effects
10. Get a Black Belt in Cognitive Techniques
11. Create Meaning in Your Life
12. Increase Your Sense of Achievement
13. Learn Meditation, Mindfulness and Self-hypnosis
14. Learn to Love Yourself

I recommend that you quickly skim through the book and highlight the parts you find most interesting. It will be motivating to read the book and see that it is full of useful measures and techniques you can try. Afterwards, go through the book once more, slower this time, and follow the techniques and the program, step by step.

In order to make it easier for you to follow the program and do the exercises, I have created several tools. One such tool is the Workbook accompanying this book (available on Amazon); it is simply titled *14 Steps to Happiness - Workbook*. Another one is the digital system I have made accessible at kristianhall.com/system. If you sign up on the site, you will receive a weekly email in your inbox with instructions and reminders about your weekly tasks. In those emails there will also be a motivational video for each step, where I give further instructions. These videos are also available on YouTube.

Regardless of whether you read through the book quickly once and then follow the program step by step, or whether you begin straight away during your first read, the aim is that you follow one step per week. If this feels too fast, you can take two weeks, or even a month, per step[2]. During the week of a given step, read the chapter thoroughly while you complete the suggested exercises.

At the very end of the book, you will find a weekly schedule that will help you complete the program. Look it up now, so you can see how to combine the different steps. I have included a print-friendly version of this form on my website, kristianhall. com, under *Resources*.

Getting rid of depression is mostly about changing habits. It is about learning to live life in a different way, learning to think in a different manner, and to be active in ways that lead to a better balance in your emotional life. In order to achieve this, you must work along two dimensions. One dimension is *what you do*, and the other is *how you think*. The first one is easier to deal with than the second. That is why the first chapters are about what you do. Gradually, we will introduce elements of how you think.

Changing habits is not always easy. Most of us will at some point try to change some of our habits, without this necessarily

---

[2] For the sake of simplicity, I write *week* in relation to this time period, which might in your case be two weeks or more.

being successful. How many people have signed up for a gym membership with a 12-month contract, and ended up using it only once a month or even less? One of the reasons it can be so hard to change habits is because, in a way, you are working against yourself. Habits are laid down as hard-wired, neural connections in the brain, and it is only natural that it takes time to change them. In some cases it can take months, maybe even years. This is not necessarily a positive message, but it is the truth. It is much better to embrace a hard truth than to end up disappointed and without progress.

Changing habits is plainly and simply about repeating the new habits you wish to encode into your brain, frequently enough for them to stick, while you let the old, bad habits die off by simply not doing them. Each time you perform an activity or a sequence of activities that you wish to turn into a habit, it will be encoded into your brain. With enough repetition, it will stick. You will learn how to change your habits in the chapters that follow. We will start with diet, training and exercise, and activities linked to positive emotions. We will continue by looking at how you can improve your sleep, and how to go through therapy most efficiently. Then we will look at how gradually increasing your sense of gratitude can help you hold on to the good aspects of your life. After this we will look at how people can be both the best and the worst aspects in life. You will learn about triggers and different cognitive techniques. I will show you how you can increase the feeling of purpose and sense of achievement in your life, and how you can resolve practical problems. Finally, we will explore different forms of meditation, mindfulness and self-hypnosis, before we finish with how you can accept yourself to a larger degree and eventually love yourself more.

Although the steps are presented in a sequence, focusing on one step at a time, all the different steps can have an impact on other steps. For example, improved sleep (Step 5), will lead to more energy and better concentration, which in turn will increase your sense of achievement (Step 12). One of the measures to improve sleep is exercise (Step 3). Keep this in mind while you are reading the book.

Another essential principle is that we are all different. If you feel that the techniques and measures in one of the steps are not relevant for you, or are not working, *simply ignore them and move on.* There are no universal keys that will unlock all shackles of depression, but there are research-based measures you need to explore before you can know whether they will be useful for you.

Your most important task going forward is becoming a detective in your own life by identifying what really works in your very specific case. The way to succeed at this is to try a lot of different things, and keep what works! This book will give you 14 different ways to tackle depression, and I am confident you will find many angles that will work for you.

Something that may prove to be of fantastic value to you in this work is to get a diary, and use it. My first book, *Rise from Darkness*, originated from me using many volumes of notebooks and diaries to record what specifically worked for me in my work to get well, and what didn't.

By keeping a diary or journal, you can systematically reflect and record your own thoughts and conclusions on which measures, techniques, and steps are most relevant to you. You can also write about your own mental processes and automatic thought patterns. This will become crucial information for you in order to identify your demons, so you can later conquer them. It's like the great General Sun Tzu wrote: *If you know the enemy and know yourself, you need not fear the result of a hundred battles.*

Eliminating negative, harmful patterns of thought and behavior starts with knowing how they operate, where they originate and how they develop. A diary will be an extremely useful ally in this work.

There are many roads that can lead to depression. For some, life takes a wrong turn and after that, everything goes downhill. Maybe you get diagnosed with an illness that makes life more difficult, or maybe you lose your job. Or, as in my case, a loved one passes away.

Another common reason is the gradual development of a poor self-image, often starting with bullying at school or parents putting high pressure on academic achievements.

When working to get rid of depression, it can be useful to know the cause of it. The reason for this is that some forms of depression should be treated differently to others. If you are unable to pinpoint specific reasons for your depression, your illness could be caused by biological factors. In that case, getting medical treatment might be necessary and more helpful than for those whose depression is linked to life experiences.

If the main cause of depression is poor self-image (which is also a common consequence of the illness), and you constantly ridicule yourself and give yourself a hard time, you will likely benefit greatly from using cognitive techniques. They work directly on the hyperactive, critical inner voice that keeps putting you down.

If you have experienced trauma, like abuse, violence, illness or death, it might be of particular benefit to look at gratitude exercises. They are all about holding on to the aspects of life that are good, in spite of everything that is painful and regardless of what baggage you have. This is not necessarily done in an instant, but is possible to achieve over time.

We cannot change the past. However, we can do something to positively change the days going forward. We have the power over our lives from this moment on, until we die. Ultimately, it is up to us whether the rest of our life continues to be painful, or if we manage to turn it in a positive direction.

Depression can be a side effect of conditions like cancer, Alzheimer, diabetes, epilepsy, heart, vascular and autoimmune diseases. Having a serious disease can be traumatic in itself and can generate grief reactions, or the underlying disease can alter the body's biochemistry in such a way that depression develops. It is therefore vital to visit your doctor and take the relevant medical tests in order to determine whether there is anything physically wrong or not.

Although it is useful to know *why* you are depressed, you should not focus too much on the cause. You will not be happier by thinking about and dwelling on whatever has caused your depression; rather, you will get more upset, more frustrated and simply sadder. You will, however, become happier by following the program in this book. It focuses on what you will work *to achieve*, not what you want to get *away from*.

Life can be complicated, and often there are several causes of depression. This is one of the reasons this book contains 14 different steps. The best you can do is to try many different techniques, and keep and further develop those that work.

WHAT ABOUT ANXIETY?

Anxiety and depression are often comorbid – they come together. Anxiety can reduce your ability to think clearly as the brain's reaction to fear goes into overdrive. When faced with a threat such as an aggressive drunk man in a dark alley, the part of your brain called the amygdala takes control of your reactions. This is the so-called *fight or flight* reaction. The stress hormones adrenaline and cortisol are flushed into your bloodstream, your pulse increases, and your muscles get access to more energy. Functions not vital to survival here and now, such as the immune, digestive and reproductive systems, get reduced blood flow and energy, and they are largely turned off while the stress reaction is active.

This is a useful mechanism that can mean the difference between life and death in a crisis. It is this mechanism that makes you run out of a burning house or lift a concrete beam off someone to free them. But in some people, this mechanism goes into overdrive and is activated even when there is no life-threatening situation occurring. This is anxiety.

Some people suffering from anxiety find themselves in an almost continuous *fight or flight* mode, where they have chronic high levels of stress hormones like adrenaline and cortisol. This can have several negative effects, both physical and mental: poor immune system, digestive problems, muscles tightening and becoming sore and stiff, which in turn can lead to headaches and problems with bones and joints.

Situations which, for a healthy person, appear normal and completely safe, can trigger serious anxiety attacks in an unwell person. It could be something as simple as being in a small room, in an open space, or having social interactions. Exactly what triggers anxiety attacks varies greatly from person to person.

The good news is that the treatment of anxiety and depression overlaps to an extent. This means you can read this book and benefit from following the program, even if your main problem is anxiety and not depression. If anxiety is a bigger problem for you than depression, you will also benefit from exposure therapy, gradually getting used to and managing situations that trigger your anxiety.

Both exercise (Step 3) and meditation (Step 13) help reduce the level of stress hormones in your body. Furthermore, it is essential to get enough sleep (step 5) if you suffer from anxiety. Cognitive techniques (Step 10) are important in order to learn to recognize normal and safe situations, thus achieving a feeling of control and safety.

Many people suffering from depression also have anxiety. You do not necessarily need two completely different treatment regimens to tackle your anxiety and depression separately. All you need is to follow the program in this book while you follow the advice from your doctor, psychiatrist or therapist.

WHAT YOU DO AFFECTS HOW YOU FEEL

It is crucial that you are aware of what you are doing and which activities you spend time on. This because different activities affect the production of two groups of chemical substances in the body: hormones and neurotransmitters.[3] Let us call these substances *signal substances*, as they act as the messengers of the

---

[3] See Appendix A for a dictionary of professional terminology.

body. Your feelings are largely a result of the mix and concentration of these substances. Since you can impact the production and concentration of the signal substances by spending more time on activities like exercise, you can increase your level of control over your feelings.

The body's nervous system consists of roughly 100 billion nerve cells, also called neurons, the majority of which are in the brain. A neuron looks like a tree, with branches at the top (called dendrites), and roots down the bottom (called axons).

Every nerve cell can be connected to several thousand other nerve cells. A connection between two or more nerve cells is called a synapse. Electro-chemical signals run between nerve cells, from the brain to the body's organs and back again. In order for a signal to pass from one nerve cell to another (over the synapse), we need chemical substances called neurotransmitters. If two nerve cells in a synapse are like two sides of a fjord, the neurotransmitters can be seen as the ferries that carry information across the fjord. Important neurotransmitters for our mood include dopamine, noradrenaline, and serotonin.

Hormones work differently, although some transmitters work as both hormones and neurotransmitters. Hormones pass through the body, predominantly through the blood. They are produced primarily in the endocrine glands, like the thyroid, pituitary and pancreas. You might have heard of hormones such as adrenaline, insulin, estrogen and testosterone.

The neurotransmitter serotonin is linked to our mood and is likely to play a part in depression. Because of this, several anti-depressants work by blocking the re-uptake of serotonin in the synapses, so that the level of available serotonin increases. Increased release of hormones such as endorphins and oxytocin creates a sense of well-being. Endorphins have an effect similar to opiates like heroin and morphine (although at a much-reduced level). They can induce a feeling of euphoria as well as acting as painkillers.

Dopamine is a neurotransmitter which, amongst other things, regulates the brain's reward system. Each time you experience a feeling of well-being after eating or drinking something you enjoy, dopamine is at play. It is also central in feelings of victory and success, like when you score a goal in soccer. At the same time, dopamine has a dark side, as this neurotransmitter is involved in all forms of addiction.

In addition to all of these, there are several other important hormones and neurotransmitters that impact how you feel. Here are some examples: Testosterone is linked to male sex drive, and estrogen to female sex drive. A neurotransmitter called GABA has several functions, including reducing stress and fear. Melatonin is a hormone that helps regulate our sleep cycles.

Many activities lead to an increased production of the transmitters that are linked to positive feelings: exercise, dance, singing, listening to music, practicing music, spending time with people we like and spending time with animals. These activities lead to an increased production of serotonin, endorphins and oxytocin, all of which are linked to positive feelings. Both exercise and meditation decrease stress hormone levels such as adrenaline and cortisol, which are linked to both anxiety and depression.

The dimension of *what you do* is about spending more time on these positive activities. They will have a direct, positive impact on your emotions and well-being. The first steps in the program will help you with this.

Let us do an experiment, right here and now. Put down this book and jump up and down ten times (do not do this if you have a medical condition for which this would not be advisable).

Did you do it? How do you feel? Your pulse has likely increased, and you are little out of breath. You might not feel *better,* but you will, at the very least, feel *different.* Albeit in a small way, you are in fact a different person now than you were before you jumped, because your body has started the production of a different mix of signal substances. This is the effect we will take advantage of a bit later on in this book, by doing activities that change the levels of these important signal substances.

You Can Change How You Think

Picture the brain as a big forest, where different paths and roads are crisscrossing each other. A forest trail often begins as a game trail (animals are good at finding the best way through a forest), which people then also start using. As more and more people use the trail, it gets wider and becomes more prominent. In the end it might become a road. A trail no one uses, on the other hand, will gradually become overgrown and disappear.

Your brain works in a similar way. The more you think a certain thought or do a certain activity, the more solid the encoding in the brain will become, because of the neurons connecting with each other. All learning happens in this way. Repetition is necessary for a new habit or piece of knowledge to become established. As an example, when you learn to swim, neural connections will gradually form in the brain and become more prominent. In the end, they are so prominent that you no longer need to concentrate when swimming. The skill of swimming has become automated and your subconscious has taken over. Old habits not adhered to will disappear, just like the overgrown forest trail.

As I have experience of both being completely healthy as well as deep in depression, it is clear to me how different the way of thinking in healthy people is compared with depressed people. There are big differences. These differences in ways of thinking result in the depressed person not feeling understood. They feel that their environment is unable to relate to their feelings.

A depressed person lives in a horrible bubble, coloring everything black and grey, and distorting the sense of self, surroundings, the world, and the view of the future.

Many people suffering from depression have an inner critic,[4] which is saying things like:

You'll never succeed at anything
You're ugly
No one likes you
You'll never get a boyfriend/girlfriend

There are several reasons a voice like this can appear, including growing up with one or more overly critical caregivers or parents. Receiving excessively negative comments from parents or other people of significance can be very damaging for anyone's self-image.

---

[4] Some people hear someone else's voice, not their own. In some cases the voice belongs to someone they know, like a deceased father, others hear the voice of a complete stranger. Psychologists and other professionals sometimes categorize the experience of hearing such external voices as psychosis or schizophrenia. For this reason, it is a good idea to contact a psychologist or psychiatrist if you are hearing voices that are not only your own critical thoughts. In the text from now on, I will relate to the concept of your own inner critic, i.e. your own thoughts.

Perhaps your parents did not *see* you, or were not able to tell you they loved you. Such a childhood can result in low self-esteem and even self-loathing, in the form of an inner, critical voice, keeping you down.

A third, common reason is bullying, which increases the risk of depression.

If many people around you treat you badly for a long time and say mean things to you, then you will, after a while, start listening to them. Gradually, you will start to participate in this bullying by talking yourself down.

A voice like this can start out like one of your own thoughts. You start doubting yourself, due to one or more of the reasons stated above. Gradually, the feeling of doubt increases and morphs into self-loathing. What started as an inner dialogue turns into an evil monologue. When such thoughts have taken root, they increase in frequency. After a while, the critical thoughts become so frequent and intense that they almost take on a life of their own.

A thought repeated often enough will, over time, become almost automated in your mind, due to the neural connections associated with the thought being reinforced every time it is repeated. Neurological research has established that *neurons that fire together, wire together.*

The problem with the voice, or thought, is that you start believing it, and when you do, your already frail self-image will get damaged even further. First, you need to understand that what the voice is telling you is, for the most part, a lie. By systematically asking the voice critical counter-questions, you can reveal the lie, and when repeated over time, the voice will gradually lose its power. Eventually, it will disappear. I know this is true, because my own hyperactive inner critic is more or less completely gone. What is left is a healthy skepticism to ideas and thoughts I might have.

Skills require maintenance. If you have not driven a car in years, it will feel awkward when you go back to it. *Use it or lose it.* Painful, automated thoughts you are not using will gradually disappear, because neural connections associated with those thoughts are dissolving, little by little. This is an important part of why it can take time to get better. You simply have to give your brain enough time to change the neural connections. However, every step you take will lead you closer to a healthier neurobiological system and a better mood.

Three Fundamental Principles

There are some principles that are important to follow when getting out of depression. Here are three fundamental ones that should make up an important part of your work of getting better:

1. Divide up your work into small parts

When you want to get rid of depression, the toughest part is the beginning. The illness attacks those aspects you need the most in order to get better. It wreaks havoc on sleep, self-image, energy levels, drive and clarity of thought – all the good forces needed in order to get started on the work of getting better.

But do not despair. There is a key to overcoming this problem: *Take one small step at a time.*

Since it is a big challenge and you do not have the best starting point, it's sensible to move slowly to begin with. In this way you can work on your depression without losing hope.

Let me give you an example relevant to my own journey. Writing a book is a demanding project that can take a long time to complete. One reason many people give up when facing a big task like this is that they become overwhelmed thinking of all the words that need writing and all the editing and proof-reading work that comes with it. If you picture writing a book as one massive job, it simply becomes too much.

The secret is to focus only on one little part at a time; for example, one chapter, or even just one sentence. You write one sentence, then you write another. You write a little every day, or every week. Then, as time goes by and weeks turn into months, one day you have written a whole book!

You can divide the project of getting rid of your depression into many small parts, and focus on one at a time. You can focus on one technique or one day at a time.

2. SET REALLY LOW AMBITIONS AT THE START

Picture two young boys, Ben and Oscar, both training to become high jumpers. They have two different coaches. Ben's coach places the bar at two meters (6.5 feet). Ben knocks down the bar, and the trainer puts the bar back at two meters. Every time Ben jumps, he knocks down the bar, and every time, the coach puts it back at two meters.

Oscar's trainer, on the other hand, has another strategy. He starts by placing the bar at 30 centimeters (11.8 inches), which is an easy height, even for a beginner. Then he ups it to 35 centimeters, then 40, and so on. After each successful jump, he increases the bar height five centimeters.

Which of the two high jumpers do you think will make the biggest weekly progress? Which of the two do you think will give up on the training after a short time? And who do you think will clear the two meters first?

In the book *Tools of Titans,* Tim Ferris describes a similar strategy. A well-known Zen Buddhist teacher recommends those wishing to learn meditation to aim to take one deep breath per day. Not to meditate for ten minutes every day, but to take one, single, deep breath. A bodybuilder gives similar advice: Aim to do one push-up every day. When you have done one push-up, you will likely do another, as you are already in position.

Setting a goal and then failing can be very demotivating, particularly for those suffering from depression. But if the goals are so simple to reach that you succeed most of the time you try to reach them, you will gradually build up your self-esteem, your sense of achievement, and the motivation you need to keep on working.

Every time you reach a goal you have set for yourself, or every time you complete a task, you are rewarded by increased activity in the brain's reward system, at the same time as the level of dopamine increases.

I apply this principle in my own work when I write. I have a goal to reach a certain amount of words per week. If I get sick or have to travel, thus not getting as much done as I had planned, I "cheat" by adjusting the goal, reducing it. I trick myself so that I reach my goals. If I did not do this, I could end up losing my motivation to write altogether. It sounds silly, because I obviously realize what is going on. But if it works, what does it matter? Small tricks like these enable me to get more writing done, and to get it done faster than I otherwise would. You can also use these tricks to speed up your recovery.

3. GRADUALLY PHASE OUT BEATING YOURSELF UP

Self-hatred and self-loathing are very common for depressed people. In many cases, it is the main cause of, and what drives the depression. It is therefore crucial to stop telling yourself off, or beating yourself up mentally.

Since beating yourself up is a habit, stopping it is not done overnight. You need to work systematically over time to succeed. Throughout this book we will look at several techniques that will help you accomplish this.

I want you to start noticing how often you tell yourself off and what leads up to you doing so. By making yourself aware of this phenomenon, you have started the process of ending it.

As you start telling yourself off less and less, you can introduce a habit of giving yourself a pat on the back and some recognition every time you perform a technique or do something that improves your life. You will also learn this by reading this book.

READY, SET, GO!

I think most people with depression, from time to time, have this thought: *I am going to get well now!* They put on a fake smile, pretend that they are fine, use all their willpower to try and think positively and try to force the painful feelings out of the way. Because that is what we want; we want to be fine, we do not want to be sick. We want to be happy and cheerful like everyone else.

Then, when the setback comes after a day or two, we fall apart like a house of cards. Maybe we fall harder than ever before, because we tried, and it did not work. The depression just returned with a vengeance.

Then we might give up.

But if we are prepared for this, if we are prepared that there *will* be setbacks, it *will* be hard and it *will* take time, then we have a much better chance of succeeding.

The US Navy Seals, amongst the world's most capable elite soldiers, use something they call the 40-percent rule: When you think you have no more to give, you have only used 40 percent of your capacity. In other words, you still have 60 percent more to give. They have proven this rule over and over again. When they swim across a freezing bay, or walk through the desert or rainforest, having not slept or eaten in days, when they feel completely exhausted, when they have reached a point when ordinary people would already have long given up, they know they have not even used half of their actual energy reserves. They know, because thousands of elite soldiers before them have proven that the 40-percent rule is valid.

This rule is valid for all of us! You and I can use this as well. By convincing yourself that you always have more capacity than you think, you can get through the most horrendous stages of life, as long as you have an important goal to work toward. This is exactly what you will do!

This is the attitude I would like you to adopt. You, reading this right now. You have an illness that has ruined so much, that has reduced your quality of life and robbed you of so much joy. Your illness will fight against your recovery. It will give you setbacks, try to take away your hope, your will and the strength you need to continue your recovery work.

If you are prepared for this, prepared that it will be difficult, that it will take time and that there will be setbacks, then you can spit in the face of depression when it rears its ugly head. Remember that thousands of people before you have managed to clear the dark cloud of depression. They have recovered or, at the very least, greatly improved their lives. There is no difference between you and them. They were prepared for difficulties and so are you.

Create a strong vision of yourself, freed from depression. Picture, with all your passion and feelings, your life when you are free of depression. Decide where you are going – to a life filled with much more joy and happiness – no matter how long it will take and regardless of the difficulties you will encounter along the way.

You have a secret helper now. You have this book. Use the techniques and the program in this book continuously and every day. It does not matter if you are unable to follow the program for a day, a month, or even a year. You can pick it up and continue once you have the strength.

Remember that the key to reaching any goal is to divide it up into many small tasks or actions. Then you take it forward, step by step. Everyone can do this. You can do it too.

Now, my friend, take my hand – and let's go!

CHAPTER SUMMARY

- Work along two dimensions when you are getting rid of depression. One dimension is what you do, the other is how you think.

- Getting rid of depression is about changing habits, whereby you let old, bad habits go, while establishing new ones that support a better mood and more joy.

- Knowing what is causing your depression is useful as you can then tailor the program and focus on the measures that are related to your specific situation. But do not dwell too much on the cause(s) of the depression, as this is likely to lead to more painful emotions.

- Anxiety and depression often go hand in hand. Fortunately, they can to a large degree be treated with the same techniques and measures. You can find all these techniques and measures in this book. If anxiety is your main issue, there are excellent self-help books for that too.

- Self-help, like the measures you can find here, is meant to be used as a supplement and not as a replacement for traditional treatment like medication and therapy. Follow the advice from your doctor, psychiatrist and your therapist, and work with the program by yourself in parallel.

- Change is toughest in the beginning. In order to conquer the first obstacle, it is wise to focus on only one thing at a time and to lower your ambition level as much as possible.

- The road out of depression is not straight – it is a rollercoaster going up. It will take time and you will experience setbacks from time to time. If you are prepared for these setbacks and know what do to when they arrive (simply get back up when you fall and continue the program), you will have a much better chance of succeeding.

14 STEPS
OUT OF DEPRESSION

Step 1:

DECIDE TO GET BETTER
– AND BELIEVE YOU CAN

Look up from the book for a moment. Notice where you are sitting, your surroundings, sounds, and other environmental factors. You have now started this program and this moment might become a major milestone in your life. And that is worth taking note of.

The most difficult part of the journey out of depression is the beginning. In order to get better, you need energy, hope, drive, self-esteem, good sleep and clarity of mind. Herein lies the ugliest part of this illness – depression robs us of exactly these forces.

Luckily, there are several tricks to overcoming this phenomenon. We have already looked at a couple of them: Take one step at a time and make sure that these first steps are so small that you can accomplish them no matter what.

Here are two more:

DECIDE TO GET BETTER.
DARE TO BELIEVE THAT IT IS POSSIBLE.

Imagine you are trying to lift a weight so heavy that it is at the very limit of what you are capable of. What do you think will happen if you try to lift the weight, thinking that you will never be able to do it? What do you think will happen if you decide that you will lift it, no matter what?

Think about George Meegan, the man who crossed North and South America on foot. When his feet were aching the most, when he walked the most monotonous parts of the journey, how important must his goal have been for him: setting out to actually walk the longest journey in the world?

We all know of examples where "having truly decided to do something" made all the difference. For example, when a terminally ill woman decides to live until her daughter's wedding, before letting go and leaving this world. She is able to keep herself alive up until the big day by pure willpower, by deciding to live.

Many people believe that a person is a slave to their genes and DNA, something Richard Dawkins argued for in the book *The Selfish Gene*. Presently, there is an ongoing, exciting debate regarding whether this is in fact the case, or whether will is a power in its own right that can impact what happens to us and what happens in our body. Bruce Lipton is an advocate for the latter. He has written several books on this topic, including *The Biology of Belief*.

I like the idea that we are individuals driven by will rather than genetic robots. Contemporary research suggests that our genes do not directly determine what happens to us; rather that they work more like a library, like a potential that can manifest itself, but that does not have to.

Our cells get told what to do from an external source. These messages come in the form of chemical substances that cross the cell barriers and then move into the core of the cell, where they start a process. They can, for example, tell the cell to start producing a specific protein.

Where do these information carrying signals come from?

They come from the brain. They come as a result of a conscious thought or a subconscious process (a mental process you are not aware of). These signals can come from what we decide to do.

This is the reason top athletes spend a lot of time on mental training. It is not enough for the body to be in tip-top shape. To win, an athlete must also have "a winning mindset", a way of thinking that results in the right signals being sent to the body's organs and cells, which then result in maximum performance.

For decades, the pharmaceutical industry has had to deal with a phenomenon called the placebo effect. When testing a new medicine, a test group is given the true medicine, while another group is given pills that have no medical effect. In many cases, the placebo pills have almost as large an effect as the medicine, or even the same effect.

The significance of the placebo effect is well documented. To give some examples:[5] Around 40 percent of patients given placeboes reported a reduction in headaches and more than half of the patients with stomach ulcers reported an improvement after being given placebo pills. The placebo effect relates not only to medicine. In a research program, they wanted to measure the effect of a surgical procedure on an artery in the chest. The control group underwent a fake surgical procedure, where they were tricked into believing that they had

---

[5] All examples are from Lissa Rankin's book *Mind Over Medicine: Scientific Proof That You Can Heal Yourself.*

undergone surgery. Of those that underwent real surgery, 67 percent reported improvements in their symptoms, but of those who had the fake surgery, a whopping 71 percent reported improvements!

Traditionally, the placebo effect has been viewed as an inexplicable and quite annoying effect that disrupts the development of new medicines. It is gradually becoming evident that the placebo effect is a sign of the body's natural healing ability, which to a large degree is influenced by what you believe in, or what you have decided to do.

Unfortunately, the placebo effect has an evil twin; the nocebo effect. The placebo effect is about recovering from an illness or a condition because you expect that you will. The nocebo effect is exactly the opposite. If you believe something is making you sick, or if you think that you will get sicker, the likelihood of this happening increases. These effects are significant and through research, we understand just how powerful they are.

If you are suffering from depression, you have pay close attention to what you believe in. What you believe in and what you decide to do tend to become reality. If you currently believe that you cannot improve your condition, that you in actual fact will become sicker, this conviction is important to change. But do not despair. This book contains many techniques that will help you change your beliefs.

Right now, you can start by pretending that you believe you will get better. It is a good start. Allow yourself to ignite a spark of hope and then protect that spark. It will slowly grow into a flame. Understand that it is possible for you to get better. I am convinced that the belief you have in getting better will gradually lead to just that.

You might think: Yes, that is all well and good in theory, deciding to get better and believing it possible, but difficult to put into practice. It does not need to be. Here is a concrete starting ritual you can use in order to achieve both.

STARTING RITUAL

Coming out of depression is a transition from one cognitive and emotive condition to another. In practically all cultures in the world we make use of rituals for difficult transitions. It is a good idea to use such a ritual when starting your work of getting rid of depression.

When you perform this ritual, see yourself as going through a fundamental change: Before the ritual you are *a person suffering from depression*. After the ritual you are *a person in the process of overcoming depression*. Draw a line in the sand, where the ritual marks the transition from one phase to another in your life. Going forward, you are a person in the process of healing.

Here are two suggestions for how to perform such a ritual: one short and one long version. You can also make your own and/or use ideas and parts from both.

SHORT STARTING RITUAL

- Find a time when you know you will not be interrupted. Set your phone to silent mode and turn off other sources of noise, like the radio and TV.
- Write down what you would like to change, or get rid of, on a piece of paper. It does not have to be long; a few sentences are enough.

- Burn the note while picturing that the change is underway. Make sure to take precautions while burning it, so you do not cause a fire. Here is one way to picture the change: Close your eyes, and picture yourself when you are sad, as if you are sitting in a movie theatre and looking at the image on the big screen. Let the image pass to the left and away from the screen. Then, picture a new image of yourself, in which you are happy and energetic. It is not very important whether you succeed completely in doing this, but do your best.

- Write a "contract" with yourself. Here is an example:

It is Saturday June 6, 2020. I have decided to do my best to get rid of depression. I realize and accept that it can take time and that it will, at times, be difficult. However, it is not important how much time it takes me to get well or significantly improve, because what I am fighting for is the rest of my life. It is the world's biggest reward and it will be worth all the hard work. I will use exercise, gratitude and cognitive techniques in my own recovery process. I am prepared for hardship and setbacks, as I know that these are a normal part of the recovery process.

Signed: First name, Last name

Hang the contract in a place where you will see it often, as a reminder of where you are going, or save it and make it visible to yourself in a different way.

LONG STARTING RITUAL

- Set aside time over a weekend. Clear your schedule. Start on the Friday by tidying up your room or your home.

Buy groceries for a tasty and healthy breakfast on Saturday morning. Before you go to bed, reflect on what you are about to embark on. Try to build up expectations for a whole new phase of your life. Imagine that you are closing a chapter in the book of your life and starting a new chapter tomorrow.

- When you get up on the Saturday, take a shower or bath. Dress in clothes that have positive memories associated with them, or some new ones you have bought beforehand. You can also build in other acts of renewal in this part of the ritual, such as going to the hairdresser.

- Eat a healthy breakfast you make with the groceries you bought on the Friday.

- Then write a contract with yourself, like the one above. Keep the contract.

- It is now time for a trip. What you do is up to you, but here are a few suggestions:

- Go camping by yourself.[6] If you are suffering from anxiety, this might be too much, but it is absolutely fine to do something that is a bit scary, as it will make you remember it better and the ritual will have a bigger effect.

- Go for a walk that is longer than the ones you normally take. Getting somewhat exhausted is another way to imprint the ritual.

- Walk to the top of a mountain, around a lake, through a forest or over a hill.

- Take a picture of yourself while you are on the trip. Print the picture and keep it together with your contract.

---

[6] Mind your safety if you go for this option. Camping in my native Norway is very safe, but it might not be where you live.

- You can add several parts here; for example, describing your life on a piece of paper. You can also write about your problems while you are on your trip and burn the piece of paper, while taking precautions so you do not start a fire. Imagine that you are saying goodbye to all the difficulties in your life. You can use the "movie-theatre method" as described above, or imagine that you are waving goodbye to your old life. Another alternative is that you picture yourself walking into a hallway from a room that is grey and gloomy, closing the door and walking into another room that is colorfully painted.

- End the ritual by doing something nice after getting home from the trip. Go see a movie (preferably a feel-good movie), or go out for a nice meal with others. Give yourself a reward; you have earned it!

ACCEPTANCE

Something to reflect on while performing your Starting Ritual (whether it is short or long), is to identify the key sources of your pain. I am not saying you should *dwell* on these painful things and think about them at length (because that will only make you feel worse), but rather reflect on *what is causing the pain*.

Then, separate what you can mitigate, and what you cannot change. Decide to accept that which you cannot change, not necessarily right here and now, but sometime in the future. This is usually not done overnight, because traumatic events can create deep wounds that need time to heal. The saying that time heals all wounds is a myth. Some events will change you forever. Time cannot heal all wounds, but it will soften the experience of them.

You can also grow as a person from the painful experiences you have endured. Research shows that post-traumatic growth is a real phenomenon. It is possible to become a stronger and wiser person who can more easily help others, not in spite of, but because of, traumatic experiences endured.

It is important for me to highlight that I am not trying to trivialize your pain here. The fact is, when something painful happens, there is nothing we can do to erase the event from our history. The only thing we can do is change how we relate to the event. This is where acceptance comes in. Acceptance can be a magical process, where we face the pain head on and say: I do not like you, but you are a part of me now, for better or for worse.

When you write the description of your life in the Starting Ritual, you want to part with the painful feelings associated with your past, not the events themselves. You cannot say goodbye to events, but you can gradually get rid of the pain associated with them. The gratitude exercises later in this book (Step 7) will also help with this.

CHAPTER SUMMARY

- What you believe has a fundamental effect on your life. As Robert Anton Wilson wrote: *What the Thinker thinks, the Prover proves.* So, start believing that you can get better, even if you have to fake it until you make it.

- At the same time as you are gaining the belief that you can get well, decide to do what you can to get better.

- All big changes in life can be made easier with the help of a transitional ritual. You can perform such a ritual and decide to do what you can to get better.

- Acceptance is an important part of the process of improving your life. You can, over time, accept what has happened to you, and let go of painful events from earlier in your life, while you leave behind the pain connected to these events step by step. The Starting Ritual can help you get started with this process.

TASKS THIS WEEK

- ☐ Sign up for the email series on kristianhall.com/system, to receive a weekly email with instructions and reminders about this program. There are also weekly motivational videos included in this series.

- ☐ Perform a start-up ritual. It does not have to be big and complicated.

- ☐ Write in your journal about the fact that you have decided to do what you can to improve your life.

FURTHER READING

Lissa Rankin: *Mind Over Medicine: Scientific Proof That You Can Heal Yourself.*

Step 2:
EAT YOURSELF HAPPY

I am certain that once you have completed the ritual from Step 1, you will feel that something has changed. In Step 2, we will take a closer look at feelings and how we can influence them with our diet.

Feelings are largely about chemistry – neurochemistry, to be exact. The different hormones and neurotransmitters connected to positive feelings are all made up of chemical compounds.

All the building blocks in the body come from what we eat and drink (a small part is also absorbed by the skin). This makes diet something that cannot be ignored if we want to get rid of depression. You have to make sure that your diet consists of plenty of those nutrients that help create a better mood.

One example is the research indicating that depression can be linked to low levels of vitamin D. In my home country of Norway, many people have insufficient levels of vitamin D due to the low amount of sunshine during winter. Make an appointment with your doctor to get your vitamin D levels measured if you think your levels might be low, especially if you live in an area with less sunshine. All it takes is a blood test. Your doctor can also help you with a dietary supplement and setting up a suitable dosage, should you have a deficiency. While you are at your doctor's, make sure to talk to him or her about your depression. Your doctor may be able to help you in several ways, like prescribing medication or finding a suitable therapist.

I recently went to the doctor myself, as I was feeling lethargic and tired. A blood test showed my vitamin D levels were low. My doctor helped me get the dosage for my supplements right and, after a few months, I now have noticeably more energy.

Omega-3 fatty acids are another supplement that, according to studies, is showing promising results in relation to depression. This is not really surprising, considering the brain consists largely of fat and the concentration of Omega-3 fatty acids in your brain is high. Different people will naturally react differently to Omega-3 supplements, but I do not think you have anything to lose by giving them a go, especially considering all the other positive effects this nutrient has.

In addition to being beneficial for mental processes, Omega-3 fatty acids contribute to reduced inflammation (for example arthritis), as well as preventing cancer and heart and vascular diseases.

In his book, *The Depression Cure*, Doctor Stephen S. Ilardi recommends a daily consumption of 1000mg (1g) of Omega-3 fatty acids, in capsules or as fish oil. The Norwegian Directorate of Health, and the Norwegian Institute of Marine Research (IMR), recommendations are 800mg for women and 1000mg for men. Choose a high-quality supplement, where the fish oil is treated in such a way that potential heavy metals or other pollutants have been removed.

You can buy a bottle of cod liver oil or Omega-3 capsules. It is likely to take at least two weeks before you start noticing any effects of these supplements, so I recommend you try them for at least a month. Carry on using them if you notice improvements in your mood and/or energy levels.

Another important thing for sufferers of depression is to keep your blood sugar levels balanced. If you do not, you will have inner fluctuations where your blood sugar goes up and down like a yo-yo.

The food we eat is broken down into each single nutrient, and sugar is one such nutrient. How quickly the food is broken down depends on what you eat. If you eat white bread or chocolate, the sugar will be released into your bloodstream very quickly. The body reacts to the extra sugar by starting to produce insulin. Insulin reduces the blood sugar levels, which can make you tired and lethargic. If your blood sugar levels fall, the body starts signaling that you need energy, which in turn can make you eat more sugar-rich foods. If you then give in and eat more chocolate or other sweets, you start another cycle like the one described above.

It is natural for humans to find it difficult to stay away from sweets. We are built to be hunters and gatherers. During the stone ages, it was good for us when we found a tree with sweet fruit, as they could be few and far between. Evolution has made it so that we experience a dopamine release when we eat something sweet. This was beneficial in earlier times, but these days, with corner shops on every street and with the chocolate counter placed well within reach at the supermarkets, sugar is available everywhere. Many of us, myself included, have become addicted to sugar due to the dopamine effect.

When your blood sugar is low, you get tired. But your mood can also get low. People are different in this regard, but many of us get cranky when our blood sugar drops. I am one of those people. Being cranky can easily trigger a transition into other negative feelings. If we are cranky, we might for instance end up in situations where the atmosphere between us and other people gets sour. This can definitely act as a trigger for stronger depression.

Fortunately, it is possible to balance your blood sugar levels by being aware of what you eat. One way to regulate it is to become more aware of the *Glycemic Index* (GI) for different types of food. The Glycemic Index is a measure from nutritional physiology that defines how quickly the sugar in a food is released into the blood stream. Foods with a high GI are undesirable because they have a heavy impact on the blood sugar. Instead, choose as many foods as possible with a low or moderate GI. You can find information online by searching for "GI foods."

To avoid fluctuations in your blood sugar levels, you can gradually introduce foods with low Glycemic Index and phase out those with a high index. In practice, this involves eating whole grain bread, vegetables, meat and fish; in other words, traditional, healthy foods.

Changing your diet is not something you do overnight, as old habits die hard. I will give you a trump card, something that will help you balance your blood sugar levels and avoid a low mood due to low blood sugar levels.

This trump card is simply a bag of nuts. What type of nuts isn't important, so choose the ones you like best. Ideally, it would be unsalted mixed nuts, with a mix of peanuts, pecans, cashews and walnuts, for example. Nuts can be expensive, and it is cheaper to buy large bags of the nuts you like and then mix them yourself. Avoid the salted varieties, but you can add a little salt yourself in the beginning, while you learn to like unsalted nuts.

Always carry your bag of nuts with you and eat a few when you are hungry. Nuts contain a myriad of healthy nutrients, including Omega-3, vitamins, minerals, antioxidants and so-called phyto-chemicals, which are healthy plant-based compounds. Eating a handful of nuts every day can help prevent cancer, diabetes, and heart and vascular diseases. You will also reduce inflammation in your body. Nuts contain a lot of healthy fats, as well as proteins, and they have a very low GI.

Since nuts also contain a lot of calories, you should not eat too many of them. The optimal amount is a small handful per day, ideally as a replacement for some of your daily high calorie intake, not an addition.

Chapter Summary

- Research shows there is a connection between vitamin D deficiency and depression. To check whether your vitamin D levels are too low, visit your doctor and get them measured. If your levels are low, you can improve them by taking supplements.

- An increased intake of Omega-3 fatty acids can improve your mood. Buy an Omega-3 supplement and see if it helps you.

- Low blood sugar can lead to low mood, lethargy and tiredness. Additionally, fluctuations in blood sugar can, over time, lead to illnesses such as diabetes. You can avoid these fluctuations by gradually changing your diet to foods with a low Glycemic Index (GI).

- A trump card to improved and more stable blood sugar levels is to carry a bag of nuts with you. Eat a few nuts when you are hungry and need a little energy boost. Nuts also contain many healthy nutrients, including Omega-3.

TASKS THIS WEEK

- [ ] Consult your doctor to find out if you have a deficiency of vitamin D or other nutrients.

- [ ] Buy a dietary supplement containing the recommended dose of Omega-3, such as cod liver oil. If your doctor found a lack of other nutrients, buy additional dietary supplements as per your doctor's recommendations.

- [ ] Take the supplements every day.

- [ ] Eat at least a handful of vegetables every day.

FURTHER READING

Stephen S. Ilardi: *The Depression Cure: The 6-Step Program to Beat Depression Without Drugs*

Step 3:

EXERCISE YOUR WAY
TO HAPPINESS

There is a strong link between diet and the theme of Step 3 – Exercise. When they increase their amount of exercise, many people feel a physical need to eat better, wanting to give the body what it needs to recover. With regular exercise and a healthy diet, you will have established the best starting point to boost your mood.

Training and exercise release a myriad of positive health effects. It is important for everyone to exercise, especially those suffering from depression. This is because physical activity works directly to improve your mood. When we are active, and particularly when our pulse increases to 130-150 beats per minute, the body produces endorphins. Endorphins are the human body's own happy pill, alleviating pain as well as inducing a feeling of euphoria. Endorphins can trigger what runners refer to as the *runner's high*. In addition, the production of the body's own natural cannabinoids increases, which impacts the mood by stimulating receptors linked to an increased feeling of well-being.

Exercise also leads to an increase in heart rate variability (HRV). The heart rate variability is defined as the heart's ability to vary the pulse over a relatively short time period. A healthy heart has high heart rate variability, and this is linked to lower levels of stress, more willpower and a lower risk of developing heart and vascular disease. Training and exercise also prevent a long list of other diseases, such as cancer and type 2 diabetes.

Since willpower is essential when working your way out of depression, and because willpower is reduced by depression, the fact that exercise increases willpower is particularly beneficial for people with depression.

Regular exercise also leads to better posture, as training strengthens the core muscles, which keep us upright in a good posture. With better posture and with a body that is gradually building more muscle, you will improve your self-confidence and self-esteem. Exercise also leads to better skin, so you will look better in every way.

Depression robs us of energy and vitality, but thankfully exercise definitely increases your energy levels. All of the body's trillion cells contain inner power stations called mitochondria. In order for the cells to get the energy they need to carry out the work they are designed to do, a stable energy supply is required, as well as the removal of the waste products produced by the mitochondrial activity. Training increases the heart rate, which in turn leads to an increased blood flow in the body. This results in better circulation of nutrients to the cells as well as better waste product removal. You can see the blood as the body's conveyor belt system, transporting energy and oxygen to the cells while simultaneously removing waste.

Sleep is unequivocally linked to our energy levels and the way we are feeling. Depression can disrupt a healthy sleep pattern, which again increases suffering. Luckily, exercise will improve your sleep, and hence, both directly and indirectly, lead to more energy and a better mood. The optimal time to exercise in order to maximize this effect is four to six hours before your bedtime. To exercise right before you go to bed is not necessarily a good idea, as this can make you more awake.

Many people suffering from depression also suffer from anxiety, and both illnesses often lead to high stress levels. Endless levels of worry and other negative thoughts are key sources of this mechanism. A stressed or anxious person has high levels of the stress hormones adrenaline and cortisol. Exercise has a positive effect on these levels over time.

Exercise also make you mentally sharper and enables you to better make sound decisions, both of which are crucial when getting out of depression. The mechanisms for this are increased willpower and increased activity in the frontal lobe, the part of the brain associated with logic and reasoning. Exercise leads to the increased production of a protein called *Brain-Derived Neurotrophic Factor* (BDNF), which in turn increases the production of neurons in the brain. When getting rid of depression, it is critical to create new neural connections in the brain, because neural connections are linked to automated thoughts and habits as described in the introduction. So, you need BDNF, which you get through exercise.

Increased exercise is one of the key measures I really want you to take to heart from this book, because *exercise helps fight depression and you will feel so much better if you gradually introduce more of it into your life.*

You will also receive the following benefits from increased exercise: more energy, better sleep, increased mood, enhanced endurance, lower levels of stress, stronger muscles, increased heart rate variability, increased self-esteem, more willpower and better mental clarity. It will also help prevent illness. There is a cornucopia of benefits waiting for you, and you are about to tap into this reservoir of gifts.

Exercise comes with many small and big gift bags that are fantastic for someone suffering from depression. But at the same time, everyone suffering from this illness knows that it robs you of energy, motivation and willpower. These are all strengths required to start exercising. We have a considerable dilemma here; we know what is good for us, but we are unable to get going due to the depression. How do we solve this problem?

By starting with a very low ambition level.

It is important that you set goals low enough that you are able to achieve them more or less every time. You will then get good feelings from the increased activity in your brain's reward system and from the higher levels of dopamine. This also prevents you beating yourself up in your head.

If you are in a place where your body and mind object to the mere thought of physical exercise, you can start by walking as little as five extra steps per day. In fact, I want you to put the book down right now and take five steps. Did you do it?

Feel free to start with a higher ambition level than the one I am describing here. You can, for example, set your goal to walk for ten minutes every day. The most important thing is that you set a goal that is low enough for you to achieve it, preferably every time. And then you increase it a little bit every week. Create a new habit for yourself: walk every day, whether it snows, rains, or is freezing cold.

Using a pedometer or other device for measuring your activity can be motivating. If you choose one that also measures quality and amount of sleep, you will kill two birds with one stone. Wear the pedometer for a few days without pushing yourself to walk more – just use it to measure how much you currently walk. Then you increase the ambition by 500 extra steps per day, until you have reached 10,000 steps per day, which is what experts recommend. You can find a second-hand pedometer online for a few dollars.

The great part about walking is that you can add in several elements that improve mood in their own right. Walk during daylight if possible. Increased exposure to daylight will improve your sleep, increase your energy levels and increase the production of neurotransmitters and hormones associated with well-being.

You can also bring someone you like along on your walks, so you get a social connection as a bonus. One of the simplest and best things anyone can do for a family member with depression is invite them out for a walk.

Alternatively, you can bring a dog. Spending time with animals makes you happier, makes you walk further and makes it easier to strike up a conversation with strangers, as there are few topics as easy to talk about as dogs.

Another strategy for getting more exercise is to choose an activity that fills you with joy. Many people love ball sports, like soccer or tennis. Personally, I love hiking in the mountains and forests, often for hours at a time.

Even though *what* you do is not important as long as you are doing *something*, different exercise forms have different effects.

The most effective form of exercise is aerobic training with moderate intensity, like fast walking, jogging, skiing, ball sports, swimming and mountain hiking. All physical activity that gets you out of breath is aerobic exercise. Ideally, you should keep at it for at least 30 minutes. But forget the ideal. Initially, you should set the bar very low and then gradually get used to incorporating two to three workouts per week so they become a natural part of your schedule.

 ## CHAPTER SUMMARY

- Physical exercise comes with a whole box of treasures, in the form of positive health effects for both body and mind. You get more energy, better sleep, better mood, enhanced endurance, less stress, bigger muscles, increased heart rate variability, better self-esteem, more will-power, and better mental clarity, at the same time as preventing illness.

- Aerobic exercise for 30 minutes or more is the most effective form of exercise, for example a fast walk, jogging, ball sports, cycling and swimming. Try to do two to three workouts per week. If more workouts work better for you, you can exercise as often as every day, as long as you vary the exercise to avoid repetitive strain injuries.

- If you currently do not do any exercise, start by going for a walk every day. Start with a ten-minute walk (or five steps, like you already did), and then increase it from there. The important thing is just to get started.

TASKS THIS WEEK

- [ ] Take dietary supplements and eat at least a handful of vegetables every day.

- [ ] Gradually increase the amount of exercise you do. It does not have to be more than a walk every day - preferably in daylight, preferably in nature and preferably in the company of people you like and who have a positive impact on you. You can start with short walks and gradually increase the time/distance.

FURTHER READING

Alex Korb: *The Upward Spiral: Using Neuroscience to Reverse the Course of Depression, One Small Change at a Time*

Step 4:
FIND SOURCES OF JOY

Now that we have gone through the steps that will help build a good physical foundation for the work needed, we will look at activities to help you fill your everyday life with better feelings.

Physical exercise is one of the fastest ways to achieve better brain chemistry; as in the increased production of the neurotransmitters and hormones that are associated with well-being and happiness. But there are other activities that contribute to the same thing.

Although research tells us that certain activities lead to a better balance in the transmitters, there can be major differences in the way these activities impact us on an individual level. It is therefore important that you become an investigator in your own life, in order to understand yourself better.

Below is a simple exercise to help you identify and prioritize the activities that will help you to improve your mood. I call it *A Practice with a Piece of White Paper*. Even though the exercise is very simple, later in the program you will see that it is a central part, as many other techniques are based on it.

TECHNIQUE: A PRACTICE WITH A PIECE OF WHITE PAPER

- Find a blank sheet of paper.
- Fold the sheet in half or divide it by drawing a line through the middle.
- On the top half, write down everything you can think of that gets you into a good mood, or that increases your energy levels. Also write down the names of all the people who lift you up, who make you happy and that you want to spend time with.
- On the bottom half, write down the opposite: Activities and triggers that drag you down, make you sad, angry or frustrated and people who bring you down. Make sure to either anonymize the names on the list (use code words that only you understand), or make sure no one will find the list. It can be hurtful for someone to find their name on the bottom part of the sheet.
- Going forward, systematically choose several activities and people from the top of the sheet and at the same time avoid activities and people from the bottom part.
- Work with your sheet and let it evolve over time. Erase or add items as you get better at analyzing your life, yourself and your situation. You can save the list on your mobile phone, so you always have access to it, or you can carry the physical piece of paper in your pocket or purse.

Below you will find some suggestions for activities you can try out to see if they improve your mood. There are many more of these types of activities, and since we are all different, what works for me might not work for you, and vice versa. The point is that we can all benefit from looking at our lives with a new set of eyes in order to identify what makes us happy and what drags us down.

Music

Music can either make a depression worse, or better. It is therefore important that you are aware of how you are using music. I had my own depression ritual that made me worship my own depression, made me roll in it and marinate myself completely. I used to drink some red wine, put on the saddest music I could think of (like *Portishead*), turn all the lights off, except for one candle, and lie on my bed in a fetal position. I would lie there for hours, while thinking about dying. Not exactly happy times.

It is much more beneficial to make a playlist of uplifting music that makes you happy. I have shared a playlist on kristianhall. com (under *Resources*) that you can use as a starting point to make your own list.

If you are one of the lucky ones who can play an instrument, this is definitely an activity that will improve your mood. Playing an instrument is meditative and has many of the same effects as meditation, which you can read more about in Step 13. If you play in a band you will get the added bonus of social interaction.

Song

Next time you see or hear a choir, on TV or live, take notice of the choir members' facial expressions. They are generally in a happy mood, and for a good reason; they are full of endorphins and other good transmitters like oxytocin. Several studies have confirmed that singing helps fight depression.

Those who sing in a choir also live longer than others and I am convinced this is due to all those beneficial signal substances.

79

You can use singing as your own therapy. I used to sing a lot, especially during the years when I was getting out of depression. I usually sang when I was alone, so I did not have to consider others, and I could turn up the volume on the music I was singing along to. It does not matter whether or not you are a good singer, unless singing makes you ashamed or cringe. The point of the exercise is to improve your mood and if you get the opposite effect, then singing in a choir is not for you.

DANCE

Dance is a form of aerobic exercise and this is probably the main reason why dancing has such a positive effect on us when fighting depression. In addition to being a good form of exercise, dancing is fun, and you will get the same mood boost when you dance as when you are listening to music. If you choose partner dancing, you will receive these good effects and be social at the same time. If you dance close to someone else, like in Tango or Salsa, you get oxytocin as a bonus. You will find a special playlist that is suitable for dancing at kristianhall.com (under *Resources*).

BEING IN NATURE

Being outdoors is my favorite activity. I simply love going for walks and hikes along the coastline, in the forest, or in the mountains. I experience peace of mind there. Ideally, I would go for a long walk every day, but that is difficult to achieve between working, writing books and having a family life. I compensate by going for walks around my neighborhood every day, preferably in daylight. My Golden Retriever Lily makes this an enjoyable task that is easy to accomplish, as I have to make sure she gets her exercise.

Research has shown that people living in a house with a view have lower blood pressure and resting heart rate than others. This is linked to lower stress levels. I can easily notice the effect of nature while I am out walking. I lower my shoulders, and breathe deeper and more freely.

When you are out in nature, your gaze will naturally rest on landmarks, the horizon or the trees around you. This makes you move the focus from your thoughts, which are often painful, to your surroundings. Walking in nature is a form of meditation, giving you all the good effects of meditation that we will look at later in the book (see Step 13).

DAYLIGHT

Daylight impacts your mood and your sleep patterns. Your body produces vitamin D when your skin is exposed to sunlight. Lack of daylight, on the other hand, can lead to the release of the sleep hormone melatonin, even during daytime, something that can disturb your sleep patterns. It is especially important you get exposed to daylight in the autumn and winter, as often as you get a chance. If you live in a place where that is not always possible, a light therapy lamp can be useful.

CONTACT WITH PETS

Have a cat in your lap for an hour or sit next to a dog and pat it for a while. Or go for a walk with a playful, happy dog. Notice the effect it has on your mood. Julie Barton wrote a book about how her dog saved her from depression: *Dog Medicine: How My Dog Saved Me from Myself.*

Contact with pets lowers blood pressure, prevents heart and vascular disease, reduces the risk of developing allergies later in life, reduces stress and anxiety, and increases the levels of neurotransmitters such as serotonin and oxytocin, both of which are linked to well-being.

The first dog we had was a Golden Retriever called Goldie (creative, I know). She was an adorable dog, with a sixth sense for people's emotions. Dogs' sense of smell is many times more sensitive than that of humans and it is well known that dogs can pick up the scent of various chemical compounds in the body, such as adrenaline. Our Goldie (and other dogs) could probably smell people's feelings. Every time I was down as a child, Goldie would come running, sit down next to me, and use her snout to lift up my arm so she could get her head under it. That way she forced me to lean against her and cuddle her. What a gift that dog was!

Dogs are capable of loving their owners unconditionally. The joy a dog expresses when you come home is enormous.

If you are able to look after a dog, consider getting one. But make sure you get a breed that suits you and your activity level. Being a dog owner is somewhat demanding. You have to feed it and give it regular exercise. If you are very sick, you may not be able to cope with this responsibility. But try to find other ways to spend time with animals, like visiting someone who has a dog, or offering to take the neighbor's dog for walks.

Chapter Summary

- Research has shown that there are several activities that increase the body's important signal substances which are connected to positive moods, like endorphins, oxytocin, dopamine and serotonin.

- Be your own investigator and find out which activities can benefit you. Spend more time doing these and avoid the ones dragging you down. The Practice with a Piece of White Paper is useful here (see page 78).

- Some people can be our biggest sources of joy, whilst others can drag us down. Step 8 is about friends and family and the impact they can have on depression.

- Here are some positive activities you can try: Singing, dancing, listening to and playing music, and connecting with pets.

Tasks This Week

- ☐ Take dietary supplements and eat at least a handful of vegetables every day.

- ☐ Go for a walk every day, or do some other form of aerobic exercise or movement that increases your heart rate.

- ☐ Do the Practice with a Piece of White Paper.

- ☐ Sing or dance a little every day, or do something else that gives you positive feelings.

- ☐ Listen to uplifting music. You can find playlist suggestions under *Resources* at kristianhall.com.

 ## Further Reading

Kristian Hall: *Rise from Darkness.*

Step 5:
SLEEP BETTER

The vast majority of people suffering from depression also suffer from lack of sleep. Inadequate sleep makes depression worse. It is therefore crucial to take steps to improve your sleep. This is the focus of Step 5.

Proper sleep is important for several reasons. The purpose of sleep is to allow the body and mind to repair and develop. Sleep is our maintenance time. Two stages of sleep are particularly important to the quality of sleep: the so-called REM-sleep (*Rapid Eye Movement*) and deep sleep. The former maintains the mind, while the latter is primarily for the body to recover.

The amount of sleep we need varies from person to person. For some, as little as three hours is sufficient, while others need at least ten hours to function optimally. I sleep an average of seven hours, but I have been through many periods, sometimes weeks and months at a time, where I have only slept for one to three hours every night. This is far too little for most people and results in bad moods, chronic tiredness, and frazzled nerves. I have, to a large extent, resolved my own sleep problems with the help of self-hypnosis and meditation, but there are also other measures that are effective for sleeplessness.

SLEEP HYGIENE

Good sleep hygiene is perhaps the most basic element of enabling good sleep. Sleep hygiene involves factors such as when and for how long you sleep. A multitude of studies have shown that going to bed and getting up at more or less the same time every day, including the weekends, leads to improved sleep.

Here are some tips to improve your sleep hygiene:

- Avoid drinking too much coffee and other beverages containing caffeine, and avoid all caffeine after 5pm.
- Use your bed only for sleep and sex. No working, watching TV, playing games on your mobile phone etc.
- Make sure you have a good environment for sleeping. The room should be cool and dark (blackout blinds are great). You should also limit disrupting noise (ear plugs from the pharmacy can help).
- Eat a banana before going to bed. Bananas contain melatonin, which helps promote sleep.

Many depressed people will recognize the following pattern: You go to bed, but cannot sleep because you keep thinking about all your worries, anxieties and your depression. You lie there, hour after hour, while your thoughts gradually become darker and more anxious. The fear of not being able to sleep becomes a reason in itself for sleeplessness. Eventually you might fall asleep, late in the morning. Because you fell asleep late, you get up late, and this makes it even harder to get to bed at the right time the following evening.

The Spielman method can be a good help. It recommends that you go to bed at the same time every night, but more importantly, that you also get up at the same time every morning, *regardless of how little you have slept!* When you go to bed, you are not allowed to lie awake in bed for more than 15 minutes. After 15 minutes, you must get up, go for a walk or read a book, and then to go back to bed. If the new attempt does not work, you have to repeat the procedure; get up and continue reading, and keep going like this until the night is over and you have to get up.

The benefit of the Spielman method is that it works. The drawback is that it is brutal, and can lead to some really tough nights and days before your sleep gradually improves. It also demands a large amount of willpower, as you have to force yourself to get up, regardless of how tired you are. As mentioned, willpower is something many depressed people struggle with.

If you have tried the Spielman method and it did not work for you because it was too tough, you can still use of some of its elements. You can, for example, follow the principle of not lying awake in bed for a long time. Instead, get up. By doing this, you avoid turning the bedroom into a torture chamber associated with sleeplessness. If you have got to the point where you are dreading going to bed every night because you *know* you will not be able to sleep, you have a problem. The solution is exactly what Spielman suggests; get up, rather than lying awake, twisting and turning.

See if you can turn the sleepless parts of the night into something more positive. Just imagine how many books you can finish during these sleepless hours. You can also learn to meditate and use your sleepless time for this (with the added positive side effect that meditation can make you fall asleep).

The fear of not being able to go to asleep is your worst enemy when it comes to sleep. If you are able to relax more, it will be of great benefit.

Another element from the Spielman method you can try is to get up at the same time every day, no matter how tired you are. After several nights of poor sleep, you will eventually get so tired that it will be easier to fall asleep at night.

Light, Screens and Activities Before Bedtime

Our sleep cycles are strongly linked to daylight and darkness, due to the fact that light reduces the natural release of the hormone melatonin, which promotes sleep. This is the reason it is difficult to sleep well in the summer in places like Alaska, where it does not get completely dark at night.

You can alleviate this problem by controlling the amount of light you are exposed to. In the summer you can use blackout curtains in your bedroom. During the day you will benefit from getting exposed to the daylight outdoors. During the darker months you can use a light therapy lamp. Make sure you do not spend a lot of time in front of the TV, iPad or mobile phone at night, as this light is strong enough to trick your brain into believing it is daytime, which will make you more awake. Turn off all screens an hour or two before going to bed. This will also help you stay away from activities that stimulate your adrenaline production, as this hormone is sleep disruptive. Examples of such activities include computer games, horror movies, action movies and thrillers. It is better to fill the last hours of the day with calming activities, like reading a book or listening to calming music.

As mentioned previously, training and exercise improve sleep. According to Peter Hauri, one of the world's most prominent sleep doctors, it is ideal to work out four to six hours before going to bed, as this leads to an optimal curve in the body's core temperature. It is also easier to sleep at night when you are physically tired. If you spend most of the day indoors and also if you are sedentary most of the time, it will be more difficult to sleep well.

Most parts of our lives are connected in one way or the other. The advice you got in the chapter about exercise will also improve your sleep. Attack depression from several angles at the same time, by gradually changing your whole lifestyle. You can achieve this by following the steps in this book.

As we know, many depressed people also suffer from anxiety. A main reason those struggling with anxiety often sleep poorly is that anxiety increases the levels of stress hormones, like adrenaline, in the blood. How can you decrease your level of adrenaline? The most effective methods I know are exercise and meditation, the latter of which you can read more about in Step 13.

SLEEPING PILLS

Pharmaceuticals (sleeping pills) can be effective in treating sleeplessness for certain periods of time. However, they have side effects and should therefore be used with caution and not as a long-term solution. As a rule of thumb, all addictive medication should be avoided. Sleeping pills often work best when they are kept in the drawer, because the fear of not being able to sleep can be reduced by knowing that you have "a secret weapon."

It is important you follow your doctor's orders when it comes to sleeping pills. The doctor knows a lot about increased tolerance (the need to increase the dosage over time, in order to achieve the same effect), addiction, side effects, and *rebound* effects (the sleep problems can get worse than they were to begin with when you stop using the pills), and will be able to prescribe the medication best suited to you and your specific situation. Many doctors, including Peter Hauri are skeptical of sleeping pills and only see them as a short-term solution.

DRUGS

Many people turn to drugs and alcohol when they cannot sleep. When you drink alcohol, it leads to an immediate release of dopamine, a neurotransmitter connected to the sleep system. It makes it easier to fall asleep. The problem is, though, that the increased production of dopamine is followed by a dopamine deficiency, which ruins the quality of your sleep. In other words, you are swapping one problem for another, falling asleep more easily, but getting a poorer quality of sleep. You get exactly what you wanted to avoid. Reducing your alcohol intake is therefore one of the most effective measures you can implement in order to sleep better. It will also reduce your anxiety, as alcohol is a neurotoxin that creates an imbalance in the nervous system.

Another drug that disrupts sleep is nicotine. Tobacco, as found in cigarettes, contains nicotine. Nicotine is classified as a CNS stimulant (Central Nervous System stimulant), and it reduces the quality of sleep. If you smoke or use other tobacco products daily it can be difficult to stop completely, but you can benefit from cutting down on your evening use of these products. If you suffer from poor sleep, you have now got a powerful new argument for quitting smoking or using tobacco products all together.

The last drug I want to mention is caffeine. It might be obvious, but caffeine is another stimulant of the central nervous system that inhibits good sleep. I love coffee, but I never drink it after 5pm, in order to protect my sleep.

Caffeine is also present in many forms of soft drinks, like Coca Cola, not to mention energy drinks. (If you suffer from lack of sleep you should avoid these like the plague.) Tea, particularly black tea, contains theobromine, a caffeine-related substance. Chocolate also contain caffeine, although in lesser amounts. A lesser known fact is that many medications contain quite large amounts of caffeine, including some painkillers. If you are using medication, check the information on the packaging or ask your doctor.

SLEEP LOG

We have now looked at several different factors that impact your sleep quality. It is very useful to be aware of all these different factors and how they work. In order to find out exactly how they impact your situation, you have to be more thorough. A useful tool for this purpose is a sleep log.

A sleep log is a form you fill out on a daily basis, where you rank the quality of the previous night's sleep and note down how many hours you slept. The latter is not always easy to determine, especially if you wake up frequently during the night. It is not a good idea to check the time several times during the night to keep track of your hours. It is best to settle for an estimate of how long you think you slept.

A clever alternative is to use an electronic activity tracker (for example, a Fitbit or a Garmin device). This resembles a watch and is an electronic aid that measures the number of hours spent in deep sleep and light sleep, as well as hours awake. It is also used to measure daytime activity and number of steps walked.

A great advantage with devices like these is that you might find out that you underestimate how much you sleep. You get up after a bad night's sleep and tell people you barely slept a minute, because that is how it feels and because you remember the awful hours before you fell asleep. If you had used an activity tracker, it would possibly have told you that you slept for five hours, which actually is not too bad. An activity tracker will also help you keep a log of how active you are during the day, which can motivate you to put more effort into your training and exercise regime.

In addition to the number of hours slept and the quality of that sleep (on a scale from 1 to 10), you should also keep a log of other factors that can impact your sleep. For example; how long you exercised for and when, how much alcohol you had, when you had your last cup of coffee, when you had your last cigarette for the day, how stressed you were yesterday and what you were doing for the last few hours before going to sleep.

I have created a sleep log form; you can find it in Appendix D. Print out one form per week and fill it out after every night's sleep. You can also download the form by going to *Resources* at kristianhall. com. If you consult a doctor for your sleeping problem, bringing a completed sleep log will help him or her give you more efficient help.

After you have recorded your sleep log for a while, you will learn a lot about why you sleep poorly. A pattern will likely emerge, where you can see whether it is stimuli (like coffee, cigarettes or screen use at night) that is your main problem or something else, like stress. If your sleep problems are stress related, then both meditation and self-hypnosis are really good tools to use.

MEDITATION AND SELF-HYPNOSIS

Meditation and self-hypnosis are, as far as I am concerned, the golden tools, not just for sleeplessness, but also for depression. The list of positive effects these techniques can have is long and it keeps getting longer as scientists find out more. In addition to the advice regarding exercise, I specifically want you to take this advice to heart once you finish reading this book: Learn to meditate – and practice it daily!

I suffer from a condition called *Restless Legs Syndrome* (RLS). This condition leads to a disturbance in the body's dopamine system and since dopamine is linked to the sleep cycle, RLS results in light sleep with frequent interruptions during the night.

The only things I have found that help alleviate my RLS are meditation and self-hypnosis. Some years ago I dropped my phone in a river while rafting, losing all my self-hypnosis recordings. This was followed by a two-week vacation with very poor sleep. Once I returned home, I got myself a new phone and with it I got my self-hypnosis recordings back (thanks to the automatic backup feature). When I had resumed my self-hypnosis routine, it only took a few days to go back to sleeping well. For me, this shows just how powerful this method can be. Thankfully, the recordings are now available online (e.g. on YouTube), so I will never lose access to them again.

Self-hypnosis and meditation are amazing in that the methods can be of benefit for several issues at the same time: anxiety, depression, worrying and poor sleep. As these techniques are so beneficial, they make up one of the 14 steps (Step 13).

Chapter Summary

- Depression often leads to poor sleep, while at the same time you are requiring more sleep due to the depression.

- Improving the quality of your sleep will tremendously improve your overall situation.

- There are many effective measures to combat poor sleep, like keeping a sleep log, improving sleep hygiene, avoiding stimuli like coffee, turning off all screens a couple of hours before bedtime, and meditation and self-hypnosis.

TASKS THIS WEEK

- ☐ Take dietary supplements and eat at least a handful of vegetables every day.

- ☐ Go for a walk every day, or do some other form of aerobic exercise or movement that increases your heart rate.

- ☐ Keep a sleep log (see Appendix D or find the form under *Resources* on kristianhall.com). Start to become aware of how your sleep is affected by the different factors in your life. Avoid screen time before you go to bed.

FURTHER READING

Peter Hauri and Shirley Linde: *No More Sleepless Nights*

Step 6:
USE THERAPY EFFICIENTLY

I believe that everyone struggling with depression should, at the very least, make one wholehearted attempt at therapy. As we have seen, my first two years in therapy were essential for me to start the process of getting rid of depression. Step 6 is about how you can get the most out of therapy.

If you are not already taking part in a depression treatment program, you should contact your doctor for a consultation as soon as possible. Depending on where you live, this might be the first step in order to getting access to a therapist.

Unfortunately, getting access to therapy can be difficult. In some countries, therapists are available at discounted rates, or even for free (covered by a public health system). This is the case in my home country, Norway. In other countries, most therapists work privately, and the client pays for the therapy or gets it covered by health insurance.

Depending on their circumstances, many people might not be able to afford therapy. There could also be long waiting lists in countries that offer the treatment for free, or at a discounted rate.

If the aim is for everyone suffering from depression to get help, the treatment should, to a larger extent, include self-help, in group settings if possible. The good thing with self-help techniques is that they are always available and accessible. Working on your own improvement, by following a program like the one in this book, is free (apart from purchasing the book). You can do it anytime and it does not involve travel. You can follow it at your own pace, and you can do the exercises at your own leisure. Research clearly shows that self-help techniques are an effective means in combatting depression.

But let us get back to the therapy. I have been through two rounds of therapy myself. The first time I was lucky and got in touch with a very skilled and experienced psychologist. I saw him for two years, sometimes twice a week. It was really tough, but I have no doubt that this was one of the most significant decisions I have made in my life. This therapist helped me clean up the emotional chaos I experienced after my dad's death and in relation to my childhood. During my years in therapy, I allowed myself, for the first time, to get angry with my dad. Angry because he did not manage to fix his problems and for dying on us. It was an enormous emotional cleansing to allow myself to get angry with my dad for this.

I have a mental image from this time period; it is of a huge, tightly wound knot that gradually was loosened. Perhaps one of the most important effects of therapy is clearing tied-up feelings, so you know what you are dealing with. It is easier to deal with depression efficiently if you know *why* you are depressed.

A piece of advice for when you are in therapy: remember that *you* are doing the work. The therapist is just an advisor, a guide. Someone with experience and wisdom, who can ask the right questions and help you get in touch with and sort through complicated and tangled feelings so you can understand yourself better.

Therapy involves daring to let go while you are in a session. If you are self-censoring and holding back on what you are sharing, you can end up beating around the bush indefinitely. Dare to take a deep dive into your own feelings and emotions and bring the things hidden deep down to the surface. When it is all out in the open, you might end up crying. It is healthy to experience such moments of release. Afterwards you can give yourself a pat on the back and go for a little celebration.

Since being in therapy can be very hard, it is good to split it up. After a particularly hard and deep session, it can be sensible to ease up a bit. I painted a picture inspired by the most intense part of my therapy. The picture shows a man walking on a lid, with molten lava underneath. The painting has very limited artistic qualities, but has a high symbolic value for me. It is not sensible to just take the lid off what you have kept hidden, rather it's better to carefully lift the lid, treat what comes out and then put the lid back on. If you remove the lid too quickly, it can be counterproductive and take you through a painful period.

Be kind and gentle with yourself while you are in therapy. Do not place other strict demands on yourself. Have as much social contact you feel comfortable with and avoid unnecessary stress and anxiety. The mantra is; one step at a time.

Therapists are people just like the rest of us. This means that you will experience good connections with some people and not with others. If you feel that a therapist is a wrong fit for you, find a new one. This does not mean you should quit after the first session, even if the first impression is negative, but if the connection between you does not feel better after three or four sessions, you should find someone else.

I had that experience with the second therapist I went to. He would probably be a good therapist for other patients, but he was not right for me. I discontinued the therapy after three sessions and I am very happy I did. I believe he would have led me down an unfavorable track if I had continued.

It is fundamental that you have quite a lot of patience with the therapy process. Do not give up on therapy, even if you do not notice any progress in the beginning. With my first skilled therapist, I experienced several months with little progress, followed by a few weeks with giant leaps forward. Depending on your life, your situation and your story, it is possible that you will need several years in therapy. Having said that, I believe you can benefit from stopping therapy that has gone on for years without noticeable progress, as the process is then wasted and could, possibly, also be counterproductive.

Chapter Summary

- Therapy, often combined with medication, is central in treating depression. Start by consulting your doctor, or find a suitable therapist on your own. If you have not yet started this process, you should book an appointment as soon as possible.

- Successful therapy is dependent on a good personal connection between the therapist and the patient. If you do not experience this with your therapist, try another one.

- The therapy process is dependent on you contributing to it. You are the one doing the work; the therapist is just a guide.

- Group therapy and guided self-help in groups are alternatives to traditional therapy.

Tasks This Week

- ☐ Take dietary supplements and eat at least a handful of vegetables every day.

- ☐ Go for a walk every day, or do some other form of aerobic exercise or movement that increases your heart rate.

- ☐ Keep a sleep log.

- ☐ If you are not already in therapy, or haven't been before, contact your doctor to start the process of finding a therapist. Or find a therapist yourself.

- ☐ Write every day, in a journal or something similar, about how you are feeling.

Further Reading

Irvin D. Yalom: *The Gift of Therapy: An Open Letter to a New Generation of Therapists and Their Patients*

Step 7:
BECOME RADICALLY GRATEFUL

Pay extra attention now as we embark on Step 7, which I see as one of the most important steps of the 14. In this step, we are looking at gratitude, and a special type I like to refer to as Radical Gratitude.

Radical Gratitude involves holding on to the good things in life, no matter how much pain and suffering is also present.

The first impression of this concept might be that it is provocative. But the fact that you can see only darkness, pain and the negative aspects of life, is part of the core of depression. Being depressed is like wearing a pair of sunglasses that colors everything black, removing all the joy in life.

Radical Gratitude can help you remove these sunglasses.

Everyone's life contains a mix of many elements, with grief, crises, deaths and illness on one side and good experiences, achievement, friendship and love on the other. And in the middle of these two extremes lies everything in between. People not burdened by depression are able to see and recognize all aspects of life. For people with depression, the pain overshadows the good to such an extent that the good experiences and memories can vanish altogether. Therefore, it is essential to learn to appreciate the good things, even though life may seem to include mostly pain.

American professor Martin Seligman is one of the pioneers in the field of positive psychology. In a frequently quoted study, he and his colleagues wished to identify the effects of gratitude. They asked the participants to make notes in a journal every night, of three things they were grateful for. At the same time, they were asked to rank their degree of depression by keeping a daily depression log.

Before they started the study, they expected that the patients with light to moderate depression would report the greatest effect from this process. They were very surprised when they discovered that it was, in fact, the patients with the most severe depression who reported the biggest effects. I am happy to share this discovery. It shows that there is hope for improvement, even for the most severely ill, with the simplest of self-help techniques.

I strongly recommend that you keep a gratitude journal. It takes between five and fifteen minutes for each entry. Research has shown it is best to do this either every night or once a week. If you choose the former, and you do not have enough energy to do it one night, or you forget, you simply pick it up again the following evening. After all, it is not how often you do the exercise that matters, but rather that you actually do it.

To get the full effect from this kind of technique, the key is to use it over a longer period of time, not just for few days. Ideally, you will take this short time and turn it into a daily routine that you do for months, or even years.

TECHNIQUE: GRATITUDE JOURNAL

- Get yourself a journal or notebook, or use the notes feature on your phone.
- Every night, write down three things you are grateful for at the moment.
- They do not have to be big things; it can be that today was an easier day than yesterday, or that the sun was shining.
- It does not matter if you repeat yourself. If you do the exercise every night for a year, you will write down over one thousand things you are grateful for. You will inevitably repeat yourself many times.

Another way to gradually include more gratitude in life is to express it more often. You can express gratitude both to yourself in your inner dialogue as well as by saying thank you to other people who do something for you.

Let us start with the inner dialogue. For myself, I've made it a habit to say an inner *thank you* when something good happens to me in life. I've even made it into a game to do it as many times a day as possible. This means that I express appreciation for many small things that would otherwise pass by without me paying attention to them. For example, when I make it to the bus on time. Or when I see something beautiful or funny. Or something that happened recently; when I almost ran over a cat that ran across the road, but managed to swerve at the last second. I express the most gratitude over my son; in my eyes he is a walking miracle.

It is for your own sake that you say thank you. By doing this, you create a process whereby you become better at drawing attention to events that are good in your life, regardless of how hard you otherwise feel your life is.

In addition to expressing gratitude as part of your inner dialogue, it's important to acknowledge when people do something for you. Most of us say thank you when someone makes us food or when we get a birthday present. But do you, for example, say thank you to the shop clerk when you pay for your groceries? Acknowledging small instances of kindness and service can be a powerful way to express gratitude and notice the subtle sources of joy and compassion around you.

If you add a smile and look the clerk in the eyes, the effect will be even bigger. Due to special brain cells called mirror neurons, humans are programmed to respond to a smile by smiling back. Even when it is forced, smiling will lead to the production of endorphins, the hormones I have mentioned previously that act as the body's own happiness pills.

By starting to say *thank you* more often to people who do something for you, no matter how small – and by smiling and seeking eye contact – you will surround yourself with people who smile back. The positive power of this is huge. If you do not believe me, try it for yourself for one day. Smile at everyone you meet for a whole day and observe the effects.

If it feels unnatural to smile at strangers, or if you do not like to look other people in the eye due to social anxiety, shyness or other reasons, you can begin by saying thank you without looking at the person you are saying it to, or you can drop the smile. Then, little by little, you can begin to smile more.

Since this is about changing habits, which requires repetition, it is useful to create systems that will help you remember to say thank you and smile. You can, for example, buy a stack of small adhesive stars that you stick to things you look at often. The star then becomes a reminder for gratitude, and you can stick these on the toilet door, the bedside table, the computer screen, or on your phone (which is the thing we look at most often in a day). Thus, you have created a trigger that will automatically make you smile and say thank you.

If you find it difficult to find something to be grateful for, you can actively go out and find it. I mean this quite literally. Take a walk and try to be grateful for what you see on your way. I call this a Grateful Walk; walking while looking for things you have not seen before, and where you express an inner thank you every time you see something new, something beautiful, something exciting or something fun.

As you will learn later in this book, you can reap many benefits from so-called *mindfulness*, an increased level of presence here and now (see Step 13). Grateful Walking is a version of this phenomenon, a kind of walking meditation.

You can increase your presence here and now by looking out for details you have not seen before as you walk. The easiest way is to look up, because we rarely do that. There are thousands of details out there that you've probably never noticed, especially if you are in a city.

TECHNIQUE: GRATEFUL WALK

- Take a walk around your neighborhood.
- Take the time to walk slowly. If you walk fast, you will get more exercise, but if you walk slowly, it will be easier to discover new things.

- Look up – there is likely a lot out there you have not noticed before (but remember to pay attention to the traffic).
- Make it a game to discover at least five new things each time you walk this way.
- If you see something new, beautiful, exciting or fun, say an inner *thank you.*
- Notice how the world changes over time, when you have made it a habit to express gratitude.

 ## CHAPTER SUMMARY

- People who suffer from depression will usually focus on what is hurtful and negative in their lives, in the environment and in the world. Gratitude can reverse this bias and help you take control of what you are paying attention to.

- Research shows that writing down three things you are grateful for every day can significantly improve your mood and reduce depression.

- Grateful Walking is a kind of walking meditation, which can also help you feel more grateful.

Tasks This Week

- ☐ Take dietary supplements and eat at least a handful of vegetables every day.

- ☐ Go for a walk every day, or do some other form of aerobic exercise or movement that increases your heart rate.

- ☐ Keep a gratitude journal and add to it every evening.

 ## Further Reading

Martin Seligman: *Flourish*

Step 8:
CULTIVATE THE GOOD PEOPLE

Now that you have completed Step 7, you are halfway through the program! Give yourself a big pat on the back. Good work!

Step 8 is about people, who can be our greatest source of joy. Many scientific studies have shown the connection between positive social interactions and good feelings.

We need people around us. Loneliness is a fundamental source of depression. And since depression often leads to social exclusion and isolation, we once again see one of the self-reinforcing mechanisms of depression. It is important to create and develop personal relationships that bring joy. You do not need to have many, but everyone benefits from at least one deep relationship.

The Practice with a Piece of White Paper from Step 4 (page 78) will probably have given you a clue as to who in your life is lifting you up and who is pulling you down. Make sure you do not polarize. It is not true that some people only have a positive impact, while others only have a negative impact. Most people have good and bad days, and can be spreading joy one day and be party-poopers the next. This is probably the case with you as well. We should allow our surroundings to be both, but having said that, there is a big difference between people, and it is essential to identify who is moving mainly in which direction.

In this chapter, we will take a closer look at how you can develop and cultivate good relationships, and how to avoid the ones that drag you down.

One thing to be aware of when it comes to people is that most of us are fundamentally the same. We want to have good relationships with others, treat others well and be treated well. We want to be seen and respected by others. The reason for this is that the modern human is more or less genetically identical to the Stone Age human. The Stone Age people were made to function in tribes of a few hundred individuals. They survived by cooperating. It was, for example, possible to hunt large prey, like mammoths, by hunting in groups. This is how the people who were good at collaboration survived, while those who were not, perished. Therefore, we all have latent cooperation and cohabitation skills.

At the same time, it is obvious that modern society, in many respects, has moved away from the natural state of living with others. One of the main reasons for this is that we no longer "need" each other. Especially in the cities, it is now common to engage a professional rather than to ask friends for help. This is a shame because personal relationships are strengthened when we ask each other for help – and especially when we help others. It feels good to help because we feel important.

Another sign of this social fragmentation is social media. Just a few decades ago, people physically reached out to each other to develop and maintain relationships. It was just as easy, and cheaper, to go over to a friend's and see if they were at home, than to call them. I am old enough to remember how I got on my bike and rode from house to house to find someone to play with. I didn't call or text them in advance, I simply showed up.

Today there are reports of many people, especially young people, who have few or no physical friends (also known as IRL - *in real life*), but who have countless friendships on social media platforms such as Instagram and Snapchat. I am convinced that this phenomenon in itself leads to more depression and loneliness. In fact, a study at the University of Houston shows a link between time spent on Facebook and symptoms of depression.

We have all seen pictures of a group of people, all of them sitting with their eyes on their phones instead of each other. It has become one of the best caricatures of modern society. I think we need to take a step or two back and reclaim our presence when we are with friends and family. We need to practice putting the phone away. In the house where I live with my family, we each have our own shelf where we put our mobile phones when we get home. It is *old school*, but it is effective in making sure we focus our attention on each other when we are at home.

You can suggest introducing mobile-free time in your family and with your friends. If you are in school, bring up the question at school. Maybe you can agree on some time intervals when you turn your phones off?

Put the phone away when you can – and focus all of your attention on those in the room with you.

How to Create and Develop Friendships

What do you do when you do not have any good relationships and when you feel lonely?

It is possible for everyone to make and keep friends. But you have to give of yourself. If those you want to be friends with do not think you are contributing socially, they will be less interested in being with you.

Many people who are depressed feel they have nothing to offer. Basically, such inner thoughts are usually just lies, and we will look at this in the chapter on cognitive techniques (Step 10). You may have to start by taking on the inner supercritical voice before you are able to approach other people to a greater extent. If that is the case for you, return to this chapter later, when you feel ready.

I was more or less friendless for several years. The reason was that I did not treat others very well. It was not just my inner critic voice that said so; it was actually the case. I was angry and frustrated and made negative statements to everyone. I was easily offended and took everything personally and in the worst sense. Such behavior is tiring for others to relate to, and it pushes people away.

Sometimes you have to start by changing yourself, before the friends come around.

But do not worry. Many of the techniques in this book will help you become a person who has more to offer to others, and thus becomes more attractive as a friend.

Is there a shortcut to making new friends? A trick that works in every scenario? I actually think there is.

I got my friends back, and made new friends, by consistently being someone who cared about others. Everyone likes a person who genuinely cares about others and who is a good listener. Every awkward conversation can be reignited by asking the other person questions. You can ask what the other person does for a living, what he is passionate about, whether he is active in sports or has other hobbies. You can ask where she comes from, if she has siblings, what kind of music she likes.

I like to think that I can keep a conversation going with any human being, for almost any length of time, just by continuing to ask about the other person's life. It works every time! And there is nothing manipulative about this – it is simply about taking a genuine interest in other people.

To make friends, you have to socialize with others. There is no other way. If your depression usually leaves you sitting alone, you need to create a strategy that will take you out amongst people. Often, depressed people suffer from anxiety as well, preventing them from meeting others who could become their friends.

To counteract this, you can look for places where you dare to meet others. This will typically involve meeting people individually or in groups small enough for you to cope with the social situation. You can use two different strategies here, depending on whether you already have acquaintances or not.

If you feel completely lonely and without a single acquaintance you can relate to, you will have to start from the beginning. Start by looking at and understanding who you are socially; in other words, what activities you enjoy when you are with other people.

Nothing is not an acceptable answer here, because I do not believe it. What do you like to do? The Practice with a Piece of White Paper (page 78) will have given you some of the answers. Here are some activities in which you can meet others: outdoor activities, sports, reading books, watching movies and playing music. Build social areas based on your interests.

Once you've figured out what you want to start with, you can find out what is available in terms of social activities associated with your interests. If you live in a city, it will be easier to find such opportunities than if you live in a small town. In the latter, you may have to consider traveling a bit in order to meet people you can build friendships with.

If you love the outdoors, contact a local outdoors association to find an active group in the area you live. If you love movies, search the internet for movie interest groups. The website meetup.com is a good place to start. It is a social platform for connecting people with similar interests.

The reason it is a good idea to use your interests as a starting point to get in touch with others is that focusing on a topic, rather than on other people, makes it possible to connect indirectly instead of directly. By that, I mean that if you meet a group of unknown people at the start of a group activity such as a hike, you do not have to say anything at the beginning. You can be completely silent, join the others, and gradually open yourself up for conversation. That conversation can be as simple as this:

"It's great to get out today."

"Yes, I agree, and the weather is really good."

Then you can revert to walking in silence, before someone says a few words again. The same is true with book clubs, which meet up after the members have read the same book to have a coffee and talk about it. You can sit quietly for the first few times and listen to what the others are saying. If you can sing, a choir will be a great place to meet people, because you are primarily there to sing. It is perfectly legitimate to show up for choir practice, not say a word, and then leave when the practice is over. You can open yourself gradually and carefully.

You will obviously have to expose yourself more than you normally dare to do, if you want to make new friends. You may not be successful the first few times. Therefore, it is crucial to not set your expectations too high. Instead, think of it as the beginning of a process, where you open up more and more. The principle of taking small steps applies here as well. We all end up in smaller social situations from time to time, and that is great. After all, you have decided to do what you can to make it better, and perhaps this means you need to dare to take social opportunities that you have previously avoided.

Once you have succeeded at this first step and identified a good social arena for you, and when you have visited this arena a few times, it is likely you will have met someone you feel positive about and would like to get to know better.

To achieve this, you can use the approach described above. Concentrate on the other person. Ask questions about their life; what he does for a living, what she likes to do apart from the activity you are currently doing, whether he has any siblings, what kind of music she likes, etc. Make sure the conversation does not end up as an interrogation; take it slow and try it out.

The *fake it 'til you make it* approach can be useful in the beginning of a new friendship. This technique is all about appearing to be more secure and happy than you actually are. I did this when I met Kirsten, my wife and the mother of our child, 15 years ago. There is nothing wrong with this approach; it is about holding off the more problematic aspects of yourself and your mental situation until you have become so much closer to the other person that it feels natural to bring it up.

At other times, you can break the ice by being open about how you feel. If you feel the time is right, you can tell the other person "I actually have tremendous social anxiety, but I'm happy to be here anyway", or "It's a big win for me to join this trip, the truth is that I'm struggling with depression." The best people out there will respond positively to such statements, because they will understand how difficult it is for you to be so honest, and how tough it was for you to have the courage to join the activity. After all, you are not looking to get to know those who do not accept others' conditions. Rather, you want to find the ones who may even know what you are going through because they are struggling with something themselves. (Most people do, we often just hide it well.)

A little warning here: If you meet someone else who is depressed, *make sure that you do not fall into the identification trap.* In other words, do not amplify each other's depression by identifying yourselves first and foremost as two people struggling with depression. Depression is not an identity; it is an illness to overcome.

The third phase in this method is about maintaining and developing the friendship. You achieve this by seeing your friendship as a seed that you have sown. It needs more care in the beginning than when the plant has grown and become big and strong. Developing a friendship is easier than you might think. Just act toward the other person as you want him or her to act toward you. Be interested, care about them. Contact him or her often, but not too often. (Avoid being perceived as clingy.) Suggest fun things you can do together that are based on your common interests. If you have followed the method so far, you will have asked your new friend many questions, which means that you now know a lot about what kind of person he or she is and what occupies them.

When you struggle with depression, you often need to talk about how you feel. It can feel like emptying a void. Once you have established a friendship, the other person will value being there for you (given that they are a good person who cares about others, which not everyone does). Just make sure you do not end up using him or her as a "garbage bin"; meaning that you often complain about how you feel. For a friendship to last, both parties must experience the other as one who, generally, provides energy and joy. Use the Golden Rule as a measure: Do unto others as you would have them do unto you. You would not like being with someone who mostly talks about pain and negative things. If you have a significant need to talk about your pain, thoughts and feelings, I suggest you write a journal, or find a therapist instead.

NEVER COMPARE YOURSELF TO OTHERS

As humans, we are constantly subjected to a plethora of advertising and other information that tell us there is a certain standard for what a good life should look like. For those of us who have a family, the standard can be something like this:

> You must be good looking, successful, have a beautiful spouse, two or three beautiful and well-behaved children. You have a holiday cabin in the mountains and one by the sea, and you drive there in a four-wheel drive. You have lots of friends and they are all successful with toned bodies and white teeth. You must smile and smile and radiate power and prosperity.

Most of us know that this "ideal life" is an illusion. Many lives contain parts of the above, but there is no ideal life that we should all strive to achieve. Every human is different, and a good life for me is not necessarily a good life for you.

The problem is that these messages get to us, nevertheless. Since we all fall short of this "ideal image," poor self-confidence and the feeling of being a loser creeps in. I think a lot of issues with depression in the western world stem from this.

I think this situation is particularly detrimental to young people. In our teens, we are in a vulnerable developmental phase, searching for who we are and what we should do with our lives. When external messages give us a false picture of who we should be, it can create deep wounds. Young people also experience pressure from various sources: parents, friends, school and society in general. We all have a responsibility to protect young people from this pressure, and to teach them that they are good enough as they are. I also hope that we, as a society, can eventually remove the sources of these false images.

The solution for you and me, here and now, is to recalibrate the image of what a good life is. You can create your own measure for what a good life is *for you*. Being beautiful is not important, and there are many individual opinions about what beauty is. You do not need hundreds of friends; you need one. You do not have to be the best at what you do, because it is simply not possible for everyone to be the best. Wealth is not essential either. Happiness research shows very clearly that happiness generally does not increase with wealth (as long as you have covered basic needs).

Although the recipe for a good life is highly individual, there are some general needs. Most of us need someone to share life's experiences with, both the good and the bad. We need to feel useful, have confidence in ourselves and our abilities, and feel that what we do is meaningful. All of this is fully achievable.

How do you stop comparing yourself to others?

You compare yourself to yourself.

This means to either measure your progress against what your situation was in the past, or against a goal you want to achieve.

If your depression gets worse because you constantly compare yourself to those who are not depressed, then stop and set yourself a goal of reducing your own depression. If you feel that you are lonely, take no notice of how many friends people around you seem to have, just set a goal of finding one person you enjoy spending time with. If you do not have much money and this creates negative feelings because you compare yourself to friends and acquaintances who earn more than you, set yourself a goal to gradually improve your finances.

Whatever you want to change, you can apply the principles that you will learn in this book, specifically:

- Set clear, achievable goals.
- Set a very low bar for achieving goals and sub-goals in the beginning. What matters is that you reach the goals. Do not let the best become the enemy of the good.
- Never be hard on yourself for failing to reach a goal. Just accept it and then continue your work the next day.
- When you achieve a goal, even at a low level, give yourself a real pat on the back.
- Be prepared that the change will take time (it may take years) and that the improvement process will not be a straight path upwards. Change processes go up and down and they will involve some setbacks.

Acceptance is also a very important part here. Gradually, you can start to accept that you are who you are; an individual like everyone else, with things you are good at, and things you are not good at. And that it is perfectly okay. This can, over time, grow into an acceptance and eventually a love for yourself, which we will take a closer look at in Step 14.

PHYSICAL CONTACT

The Stone Age men and women lived simply and in cramped spaces, such as caves or tents. As we became more sedentary, we upgraded to small houses or huts. People slept close together; they did not have a bed for each person.

Today, there is a greater physical distance between people than ever. We are replacing physical friends with social media profiles. By doing this we lose a part of something essential: physical contact. Humans are dependent on physical contact. It starts with the infant who cries loudly when in need of physical contact with Mom or Dad. As we get older, we gradually get used to a situation where there is little physical contact with others. Many people today have trouble receiving or giving a hug, but that does not mean the need for a hug is gone.

Especially for those who are lonely, instances of physical contact may be far apart. Those who suffer from depression are often lonely. I remember how my longing for closeness and intimacy felt physically painful during the worst years.

During physical contact, both sexual and non-sexual, signal substances that are linked to wellness are released in the body. The most important one of these signal substances is oxytocin, which has been referred to as the love hormone. In some major cities around the world, there are special cuddling clubs, where people can go to cuddle and hug other people (in a non-sexual way). There is a lot of oxytocin in a good hug.

If you are depressed and lonely and do not have a partner to hug, then what do you do? Hug your parents, siblings and friends. If you do not feel like hugging any of them, hug a dog or other pet.

Research tells us that we get an abundance of health benefits by spending time with pets. I would say that dogs in particular are great, because a dog can rarely get too many cuddles. (You can probably guess from what I've written so far that I am a big fan of dogs, even though I love my cat, Mimi, too). Being close to a dog, and especially patting a dog you love, increases the level of oxytocin in your body, lowers your heart rate and blood pressure, reduces your stress levels and makes you happier.

CHAPTER SUMMARY

- Other people can be our greatest source of joy in life, but our relationships can also pull us down and deepen our depression. That is why it is essential to prioritize and cultivate the relationships that actually contribute to positive emotions and experiences.

- If you are lonely, you can create and develop relationships by finding arenas where there is a good chance of finding someone you have common interests with. The best arenas for this are clubs and associations with a specific theme, such as sports, film, literature or outdoor life. Check meetup.com to find groups that suit you.

- If you find small talk difficult, ask questions about other people's lives – everyone loves to talk about themselves.

- Avoid comparing yourself to others; rather, compare yourself to yourself, and either measure your progress against your situation in the past, or against a goal you have for your own progress.

- Increase the amount of physical contact in your life because it produces oxytocin, which is linked to a feeling of well-being.

TASKS THIS WEEK

- ☐ Take dietary supplements and eat at least a handful of vegetables every day.

- ☐ Go for a walk every day, or do some other form of aerobic exercise or movement that increases your heart rate.

- ☐ Keep a gratitude journal and add to it every evening.

- ☐ Try to do something enjoyable a couple of days, or evenings, during the week with people that lift you up and that you like spending time with. If you currently do not have such people around you, try to identify places where you can find people like this in the future.

FURTHER READING

Dale Carnegie: *How to Win Friends and Influence People.*

Step 9:
IDENTIFY TRIGGERS AND DOMINO EFFECTS

Most of the steps in the program so far have primarily been about the first of the two dimensions you need to work with on your path to fight depression, and that is *what you do*. In Step 9 we will look at how to better handle triggers. This is a key foundation for Step 10, where you will learn cognitive techniques, which is about the second dimension: *how to think*.

Everyone has *triggers* in life. In this context, triggers mean the things that result in a reaction or a feeling, either in a negative or positive sense. An example of a negative trigger is when your depression increases in intensity because your best friend could not come with you to the movies (the trigger is experienced rejection). Or when a person with social anxiety breaks down completely, because there was no one he knew at the party (the trigger is a collection of strangers).

Triggers are important for everyone, but they are particularly important for people with depression, especially those in the early stages of the recovery process. In other words, the sicker you are, the more important it is that you know your triggers. Triggers can be a minefield, and if you have relatively little control of your emotions, which is typical in the case of depression, such triggers can put you in an emotional tailspin.

Fortunately, we also have positive triggers: things, activities and people that lift you, energize you and raise your mood a few notches. For example, when you are happy because you won $20 on the lottery (unexpected money is the trigger). Or when you hear your favorite song being played on the radio. The Practice with a Piece of White Paper (page 78) can help you identify negative and positive triggers, so you can get more of the good ones and fewer of the unpleasant ones. In this chapter we will focus on the negative ones, because a negative trigger usually has a bigger impact than a positive one. A $20 win in the lottery will not make up for social rejection.

Triggers can often trigger a chain of thoughts and emotions, which move through the mind and body with a domino effect. In addition to working on becoming aware of your own triggers, it is important that you understand the wider effects these domino effects have for you.

Here is a simple example from my own past: I was a bad loser for a long time. When I lost in a board game, I often threw the pieces and the board at the wall while cursing and swearing. Not so pleasant.

In addition to the fact that losing a game was a negative trigger that made me angry, the loss triggered a domino effect of negative thoughts and feelings. Typically things like: *I lose -> I get angry -> I say and do a lot of stupid things -> I feel ashamed of myself -> I internally beat myself up for being a complete idiot and a bad person -> I become more depressed than I was before -> I isolate myself from others.* This pattern would trigger an even deeper depression; a common example of a self-reinforcing negative spiral. I experienced many such domino effects and self-reinforcing negative spirals. I think such reactions are common in depressed people. Here is another typical self-reinforcing negative spiral I experienced, pretty much every time I was out on the town as a student: *I meet a girl I think is cute, try to make contact, but experience being rejected –> I'm ashamed and I shout at myself for being completely unattractive –> the depression is intensified –> I leave the club and go home –> I give myself a hard time for not mastering normal situations –> the depression is intensifies further.* Note that this was not necessarily a real rejection, but something I experienced as one, because I had a very poor self-image.

Such experiences led me to decline the next invitation to go out, which in turn led to greater social isolation and thus made my life even darker.

In an ideal world, you want to change yourself so that you no longer get a negative reaction to a negative trigger. But this is not realistic when you are sick and have your head full of dominoes that are ready to fall. It is quite possible to gradually change yourself so that the triggers have less and less power over you, but it takes time. And how do you do that? First and foremost with cognitive techniques, which is the topic of Step 10. But you might ask; what if I have a problem with my triggers right here and now? Then what do I do?

You avoid them.

Let me tell you about my own successful move away from being a bad loser. The first step in this process was to acknowledge and accept that I was a bad loser, and that losing could trigger oversized reactions and send me deeper into depression.

Step two was to realize that I could spare myself this domino effect, simply by avoiding playing the games.

At the beginning of the recovery process, you are very vulnerable. It takes very little to get off the track that leads out of depression. Life is full of triggers that can throw you further into the abyss. So in the beginning, you just have to run in zig-zags between these triggers and do everything you can to avoid them.

The third step is to normalize the relationship you have with a trigger. In my case, I achieved it in my relation to board games in two intermediate stages. The first intermediate step was to redefine my relationship with board games. I was able to reduce the importance of playing so that I no longer cared whether I lost or won. The negative side effect was that playing was not as fun anymore, because I did not care about the end result. The second intermediate step, which completed the process, was to allow myself to care about the game again. Now I very rarely react strongly when I lose, because I have managed to eliminate the oversized response to losing, by using cognitive techniques.

When it comes to my social anxiety, it was important for me to avoid the most frightening social situations; the typical ones were parties with many unknown people. In particular, parties where the guests gave the impression that they were "perfect" people who had mastered everything and had no problems in life. I still avoid social situations where people to a great extent put on acts. I am still very uncomfortable around superficial people obsessed with their facades who hide what lies beneath.

During my most vulnerable years, I tried to seek out safe social situations. I'd rather have dinner with a few friends than go out on the town. This worked to some extent, but I still have many memories of gruesome social events where the evening too often ended up with me depressed and lying in a fetal position under the bed covers.

As I grew healthier, I was gradually able to normalize my relationship to parties and nightlife. But it took a long time before I had any sort of normal relationship with being out on the town. I think a key factor was the inclusion of alcohol. Alcohol (and other intoxicants) act as a catalyst for negative triggers and emotional domino effects. Alcohol deprives us of self-control, which is the one thing we need to have when dealing with a difficult social situation. In this way, alcohol and other drugs act as a kind of meta-trigger by amplifying and distorting other triggers and reactions. You should therefore limit your intake of intoxicants when you are at your worst. Even if you choose not to completely abstain from alcohol for a period of time, you can choose to limit your intake to retain most of the control over your thoughts and feelings.

So how do you manage to avoid the triggers? Step one is to identify them. It is quite simple. Bring a notebook, journal or digital listing tool, and write down reflections from your day. The Practice with a Piece of White Paper will also be helpful here (page 78).

Without a doubt you will step on some of these emotional mines, because they are a part of life, even when you try to avoid them. Once you've been exposed to a trigger, and the reaction has rushed through you, try to find a quiet corner and write down some reflections. For example, if you have withdrawn from a social event and are back at home by yourself, you can take out the journal and reflect on what just happened.

What actually happened in the situation? What triggered the reaction? Why did the incident trigger this reaction? Is there a pattern here? Do you remember similar situations that triggered similar reactions?

Step two is in two parts: Plan for how to avoid the triggers, and plan for how to reduce the negative effects when you do end up in a situation that triggers a reaction.

Step three is to gradually normalize the relationship you have with the triggers so that they stop being a minefield and gradually transition to just being a normal part of life. You will come to see that you are much more adaptable than you think you are. The techniques in the next chapter will help you with exactly these situations.

CHAPTER SUMMARY

- There are both positive and negative triggers in life. The positive triggers will put you in a better mood and give you more energy. The Practice with a Piece of White Paper will help you identify the triggers.

- Negative triggers can cause a domino effect of hurtful thoughts and feelings. They are often self-reinforcing by nature.

- When you are at the beginning of a recovery process, you are at your most vulnerable and have little defense against negative triggers. Therefore, the best strategy is to avoid them until you have built up a higher degree of resilience.

- You can practice dealing better with the negative triggers in three steps: 1. Map them. 2. Plan to avoid the triggers when you can, and follow the plan. 3. Learn to live with them by gradually lessening the power they have over your life. The cognitive techniques in the next chapter are the main tools for doing this.

TASKS THIS WEEK

- ☐ Take dietary supplements and eat at least a handful of vegetables every day.

- ☐ Go for a walk every day, or do some other form of aerobic exercise or movement that increases your heart rate.

- ☐ Keep a gratitude journal and add to it every evening.

- ☐ Do the Practice with a Piece of White Paper again.

- ☐ Reflect on what positive and negative triggers are for you, and what you can do to avoid the negative ones and get more of the positive ones.

FURTHER READING

David D. Burns: *Feeling Good: The New Mood Therapy*

Step 10:

GET A BLACK BELT IN COGNITIVE TECHNIQUES

The way I see it, everyone – not only people with a mental disorder – would benefit from becoming more conscious of the way they think. Most of us go about life without reflecting too much on what is actually going on in our minds, what it means and where it comes from. And more importantly, how to change our thought patterns.

Cognitive techniques, or Cognitive Behavioral Therapy (CBT), as it is formally called, is, for me, the most basic and effective tool for changing how we think. It also makes it an invaluable tool for someone struggling with depression. In Step 10, one of the most powerful steps in the program, we will look at some basic techniques within this field.

These techniques will help you to gradually change your way of thinking, so that you are more likely to have thoughts that build you up, rather than break you down. Rational and logical thoughts, rather than adverse automatic thoughts.

One of my readers wrote to me: *Depressive thoughts can become a highway in the brain, capturing most of your attention. Let the grass grow again so it goes back to being just a walking path, and eventually disappears fully.*

Cognitive techniques are the antidote to the negative triggers and emotional domino effects we have just looked at. These techniques will give you the tools you need to stop the domino effect and normalize your relationship with your negative triggers so they no longer rule your life.

Cognitive Behavioral Therapy was developed in the 1960s and 1970s, with two American psychiatrists, Aaron T. Beck and Albert Ellis, among the most important of the pioneers. A fundamental principle of CBT is that cognitions (thoughts and beliefs) are interconnected and should be addressed together. CBT is action oriented and is used to help patients solve specific problems they encounter in life.

Cognitive techniques are what Martin Seligman describes in his book *Optimistic Thinking*, which is about how optimism can be a learned behavior. Even the most hard-hearted pessimists can, bit by bit, convert to optimism. I know this, because I once was a fierce pessimist myself, while today I am a definitely an optimist (not at the top of the scale, but well above average).

In the figure above you see my model for how thoughts and feelings influence each other and at the same time are influenced by so-called reality filters, which can also be called beliefs. If you think about your loneliness, these thoughts will create feelings of hurt. Similarly, it will be difficult to have constructive thoughts if you feel melancholy, sadness or pain. But the model is more complicated than this, because the beliefs (reality filters) you

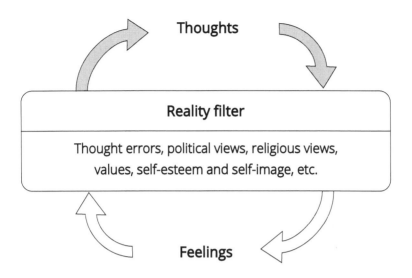

have about yourself and the world will affect both your thoughts and your feelings.

We all have reality filters, because the brain has to model the world in order to deal with it. There is simply too much information around us for the brain to handle each piece of information individually. It must create a kind of map, a simplification of the world, to which it can more easily relate.

The brain achieves this by grouping different elements into categories or concepts, such as Human, Mother, Dog, Ball etc. There are rules and characteristics associated with each of these concepts. A person's description of a given concept is in psychology referred to as a schema. A dog, for example, is a four-legged hairy animal with a tail, and this animal can bark and bite.

Even though most people have a schema for the concept Dog (those who have never seen or heard of a dog do not have this schema), there will be individual differences between the schemata of a Dog for different people.

Let us use John and Carl as an example. John was bitten by a dog when he was young, while Carl grew up with a friendly Golden Retriever who was his best friend. Their schemata for Dog are hence very different and this will affect how they interact with dogs for the rest of their lives. The properties of the schema Dog have thus become something that regulates their behavior; the schema has become a reality filter.

Reality filters can cause major damage when they are distorted in a false or negative direction. People with depression have many such distorted filters. Where I previously wrote that being depressed is like wearing sunglasses that color everything in black, what I actually talked about was reality filters. There are many such filters in a depressed person's mind. They distort the person's view of themselves, their surroundings, and the world in general. I generally believe that the main difference between those who are depressed and those who are not, is the existence of thwarted reality filters in the minds of the former.

Another reason why reality filters can prove to be destructive to us humans is that they tend to reinforce themselves. When we are convinced of something, we will look for data and observations that reinforce this belief. In psychology, this phenomenon is called *confirmation bias.* It is a central logical short circuit described by, amongst others, Daniel Kahneman in the book *Thinking, Fast and Slow.*

This is the phenomenon that the author and philosopher Robert Anton Wilson refers to when he writes *What the Thinker thinks, the Prover proves.* American psychologists Karen Reivich and Andrew Shatté refer to it as "the Velcro/Teflon effect," because observations that go against a person's beliefs do not stick, like on a Teflon surface, while those that agree with the beliefs attach themselves to them as with Velcro.

All humans are victims of this phenomenon, but it is possible to reduce the effect of it by constantly asking critical questions about one's own and others' perceptions.

The most significant reality filter we have applies to ourselves; how we look at ourselves, our self-image. If you are depressed, you probably think of yourself as something like this: *I am ugly, inept, unintelligent, a loser. I'm never going to succeed at anything.* This is a distorted and unhealthy reality filter, which forms part of the core of the illness.

The cure for depression is largely found in correcting and repairing such unhealthy reality filters. It is about rewriting the rules of your schemata for yourself and your surroundings, to make the rules neutral and realistic, and eventually positive.

Let me illustrate what this means in practice. This is how I describe my current self-image:

I am a capable person with a clear goal in life. I help people and protect the environment. I'm not a world champion in anything, but I'm good at a lot of things. I am knowledgeable and resourceful. I have many good friends and a family I love.

This is how I would have put it when I was at my worst:

I am completely inept, ugly and unattractive. I will never get a girlfriend, because no one can ever love me. I'm never going to get a better life, and I really should just end it here and now. I am a loser in all arenas.

I find many descriptions like the one above in my diaries from my worst years. For me, the examples show very clearly what depression means. When you think about yourself like that, it is no wonder you are in pain.

It is obvious that repairing the reality filters is fundamental to creating a healthy mind. How do I do that? you might ask. How can I make them neutral and objective, and remove the lies they tell about myself and about many other things in life?

Through cognitive techniques, and by adding a good dose of gratitude.

THOUGHT FALLACIES

Let us take a closer look at what the phenomenon of reality filters consists of. If you drill into an unhealthy reality filter, you will find incorrect and illogical ways of thinking, which we can call *thought fallacies*. Erroneous thinking is something that everyone is a victim of, but in a depressed person these kinds of thought fallacies often have a greater negative impact, and they occur more frequently.

To move from thinking in a way that keeps you down, to thinking so that you can lift yourself up, you need to learn to separate healthy and rational thoughts from the unhealthy and irrational ones. This means, amongst other things, learning to identify the thought fallacies in everyday situations.

Here is a list of the most common thought fallacies. You can find a short version of the list in Appendix B.

FILTERING

Filtering is the most common thought fallacy for a depressed person, and the one that is probably the most important to eliminate, because it does so much damage. A depressed person will thoroughly notice everything she does where she does not succeed, and everything which is painful and wrong with herself and the world at large. At the same time, she will ignore the things that actually do work, and the positive things in life. If, in general, you are well-liked by the people around you, but you know one person who does not like you, this is the one you'll focus on. This is filtering: you just see the negative aspects of the situation and ignore the good ones. Another example is if you think that the world is evil, because there are wars and selfish people in it. There are many more countries where people live in peace than there are countries at war. And most people are not selfish; most people wish others well.

Gratitude is one of the most effective remedies for filtering, because gratitude is about noticing and sticking to what is good, in spite of the pain.

Generalization

Generalization means putting everyone in the same box. You generalize when you say that you hate all men because you've met a man who behaved like a jerk. Or when you say that all Muslims are terrorists, because there are some extremist Islamists who resort to violence and terror. Generalization is very common; as humans we do it all the time. Since there are rules and characteristics attached to various forms, we tend to think these rules apply to all individuals who belong to a particular group. This is obviously not the case. Some dogs bite, but most do not. Some people are unfaithful, but most are faithful.

Polarizing

Polarizing is closely related to generalizing and can actually be seen as a sub-point of that particular thought fallacy. When you polarize, you divide the world into two categories: black and white, yes and no. However, most phenomena exist on a scale, not as binaries. There is no one who is either thoroughly good or thoroughly evil; we all have both sides within us. Hitler was fond of his dog. Mother Teresa had some bad thoughts. The world would be a much better place if we realized this. If we could meet each other focusing on what we have in common, instead of demonizing others. Gandhi created a peaceful detachment of India from the British Empire by understanding the perspective of his British negotiating counterparts. If he had thought "all British are evil", the detachment would probably have happened through a bloody and lengthy war.

You can counteract polarizing by remembering that most things exist in grey shades on an infinite scale, not in black and white. That goes for you too. You do not do stupid things all the time; however, we all do stupid things from time to time.

Should-ing

Should-ing is what you do when you make yourself feel bad because you "should" do something, and you do not do it. You say I should exercise, and then feel bad for not doing it. I should eat healthier and consume less sugar. Feeling bad and being ashamed for what you do or don't do is detrimental to your self-esteem, confidence and willpower. That is why I, in this book, have iterated many times that it's important that you *stop beating yourself up.* I know it is hard to do, because you are so used to doing it.

But it is time to end this now. Tell yourself that you are doing the best you can with where you are right now. You have to have patience and a long-term perspective. You should not be hard on yourself, but rather show compassion and care for yourself – which we will look at later in this book.

You eliminate should-ing by gradually replacing *should* with *can.* I *can* exercise now, but it is okay if I do it tomorrow instead. I *can* eat healthier over time and it is perfectly okay to have a treat today. You can also combine this thinking with doing *something*, even if you start with a very low level of ambition. If you feel bad for not having the energy to exercise, go for a super short walk, or do one push-up, for example.

CATASTROPHIZING

A depressed person is often prone to catastrophizing. Catastrophizing is over-dramatizing and exaggerating the effects of what is happening to you. For example, if you get a parking ticket and it completely ruins your day. It is annoying to get fined, but it is not the end of the world.

Another example of catastrophizing is when you conclude that you have no friends just because no one could come with you to the movies on Friday.

The best way to avoid catastrophizing is to put the events into perspective. Set up a scale of disaster points from 1 to 100, where 100 disaster points is the most catastrophic scenario you can imagine, like losing everyone you love while you are the only survivor. If you then compare this to everyday annoyances, you'll quickly see that a parking ticket does not even get one point.

MIND-READING

We humans can barely get a good picture of our *own* thoughts about different things. So how can we claim to know what other people are thinking? And yet we assume we know what others are thinking, both about us and about other people and subjects.

You may think you know what that boy in school thinks of you. Or you might say "my mom never loved me" and you are convinced that this is true. But how do you know? Nobody knows what other people think, not even when we ask, because people do not always tell the (whole) truth. When you realize this, and let go of trying to be a mind-reader, you can relax.

PERSONALIZATION

Personalization is closely related to mind-reading, and means that we take things that have nothing to do with us personally. Like when you meet someone you know and they do not respond when you say hello, and you think it is because they do not like you. You do not know what lies behind their lack of response in this case. She might have been thinking about something else and not noticed you, or maybe she had a bad headache and wasn't really interested in speaking to anyone.

Although we are all the center of our own universe, because everything we experience is interpreted by our own brains, we are not the center of others'. Most of the time, people are less concerned about your behavior than you think. So, if you say some stupid things when you are drunk and then wake up full of anxiety, you can relax. Although you may find it embarrassing and shameful, most other people will probably not be bothered. If you say something silly in a meeting at work, most often the other attendees will forget about it shortly after.

AVOIDING RESPONSIBILITY

Avoiding responsibility is the opposite of personalization. This thought fallacy is very similar to the victim mentality, where we have a view on reality in which everyone else is to blame for everything that happens to you.

It is true that we have control over and responsibility for some things and not others. It has nothing to do with me if my friend is in a bad mood because he had an argument with his girlfriend. But it has something to do with me if he is in a bad mood and I had called him names the day before.

Life becomes a lot easier when you understand the difference between what you are responsible for and can influence, and what you cannot control.

Put the book aside for a few minutes and take a moment to think about whether you recognize any of the thought fallacies I've mentioned within yourself. You will probably find several, such as filtering, generalization and catastrophizing. It will be very useful for you to know what these thought fallacies are and how you use them.

It is only when you know what these thought fallacies are and how they show up in your life that you can begin to get rid of them. We will look at that now, using a technique I call the Extended ABC.

EXTENDED ABC

Extended ABC is a further development of the basics of Albert Ellis' ABC model in Cognitive Behavioral Therapy. ABC stands for **A**dversity (or Activating Event), **B**elief and **C**onsequence. Becoming more aware of the basic ABCs in various life situations is often the first thing you learn on a CBT course.

Obstacles are part of life. They can be big, like when someone dies, or they can be minor and trivial, like missing the bus. The trivial obstacles are the main focus of CBT, because it is essential to be able to handle them properly. If you are overcome by these kinds of adversities, of which there are so many in life, it is difficult to live a good life.

Here is an example of such an everyday obstacle – the A in ABC: You cannot watch your favorite series on online TV because the internet is temporarily down.

Let us look at how your beliefs (reality filters) affect the reaction to this obstacle. You may be thinking: *This only happens to me* or *Everything in my life goes wrong.* Or: *Because I did not watch that episode, I'm not going to be able to sleep tonight.* These thoughts are the Bs in ABC. In other words, the beliefs and reality filters you have that affect your thoughts and feelings after an event.

It is quite obvious that the belief in this example does not benefit you. It leads to a consequence; namely that you become irritated and frustrated, and maybe that your depression gets more intense. This is the C in ABC.

Basic ABC is about raising awareness of how you react to certain events and why. The technique we are going to look at now – the Extended ABC – goes a little further, and looks at which ways of thinking would have been more useful in a given situation. To illustrate this technique, let me present the following situation:

John, a 20-year-old man who struggles with anxiety and depression, is in love with Ellen, the girl next door. One day he meets Ellen in the backyard and asks her if she would like to go for a cup of coffee with him on Thursday. Ellen replies that unfortunately she cannot, because she already has another appointment at that time.

John panics, feels rejected in the worst possible way, regrets that he asked, apologizes and runs home and hides under the blanket in a dark room. He thinks: *Ellen hates me. She will never want to go on a date with me. In fact, I'll never get a girlfriend, because all women think that I'm totally disgusting.*

Let us use the Extended ABC to analyze the situation and come up with a better way of thinking for John.

1. Let us first objectively describe what happened. John met Ellen and asked if she would have coffee on Thursday, to which she replied that she could not. That is all - nothing else happened!

2. The second step in this technique is to see if there are any thought fallacies in the way John was thinking. Can you see any?

In fact, there are many (and common) thought fallacies in John's thinking. First of all, he is *mind-reading*. He thinks he knows what Ellen is thinking about him (*she detests him*), but he cannot know that. Even if he had asked her straight out, he would not have found the answer, because as humans we often do not tell the whole truth.

Second, he is *generalizing*. He concludes that the rejection from Ellen means *all* women will reject him.

He also is *catastrophizing*, because not only will women reject him, they will always find him disgusting. He turns one feather into five chickens.

Furthermore, he is *filtering* out the negative from the situation. He focuses on the rejection and does not see that she did not say that she would never go on a date with him. She just said she could not do it on Thursday. Finally, he takes it personally, even though he does not know whether it is about him or not. He *personalizes* her statement.

It is easy to see that John has some thought fallacies. But it is not that easy to look at yourself. How often and to what extent do you do the same thing? Which specific thought fallacies do you fall victim to? It would be pretty good to be able to stop doing this, right? I'll help you with that.

3. The third and final step is to come up with a better way for John to think about this situation. Do you have any suggestions?

It is quite obvious that it would have been better for him to think that he could ask Ellen again later: Would you like to do something together with me, and if so, when would it suit you?

Let us take another example. Emma is a girl who has always loved acting and her biggest dream in life is to be accepted into the National Academy of the Arts. After the auditions, she fetches the letter with the National Academy of the Arts' logo from the mailbox with trembling hands. She opens the envelope and sees to her great disappointment that it is a rejection; she did not get in.

Emma's life collapses. Everything is ruined, she will never be an actress. She thinks: *I have zero acting talent. I will never perform again; I will never succeed at anything. My life is ruined.*

Let us apply the three steps to her situation:

1. What was it, objectively, that happened?

   She was not given a place at the National Academy of the Arts (on her first attempt).

2. Are there errors (thought fallacies) in the way she is thinking?

   She is *filtering*, focusing only on the negative in the situation. She is *catastrophizing*: She thinks she has zero talent and that she will never be able to perform again.

3. How can she think differently and better in this situation?

   Most of the people who are admitted to the National Academy of the Arts have made several attempts to get in. It is uncommon for someone to get in on their first audition attempt. There are also several other acting schools she could choose from. If she does not get into any of these schools, she could try doing something within film and television, or as an amateur actor. And if she does not end up becoming an actress, there are other ways to work within theatre and film (as a producer, director, makeup artist, special effects designer, props designer, musician, etc.). Maybe one of those could work just as well for her?

Pretty simple, right? At least on paper. But you do not go from having your mind full of thought fallacies to shaking them off overnight. It takes time and effort to learn how to think in a healthier way. It all starts with becoming more aware of how to think, and how to think in a more useful way.

In Appendix E, you will find a form you can use for this technique. Alternatively, you can find forms to print out on kristianhall.com (under *Resources*). Print out several copies and put them in your purse or in the pocket of your jacket. Alternatively, you can use a notebook or mobile phone to take notes.

If you need help practicing this technique, seek out a group to practice with, or find a therapist who is trained in these techniques.

TECHNIQUE: EXTENDED ABC

- Get a notebook, use the notepad feature on your phone or download forms from kristianhall.com.
- When something negative happens to you (hurtful thoughts and feelings), take out the form or the notebook and answer each of the following questions:
- What happened, objectively?
- Are there any thought fallacies in the way I am thinking about it?
- Can I think differently in this situation, so that my thoughts become more useful and positive?

Reduce Worries and Rumination

Most people suffering from depression also suffer from anxiety to some extent, or worry excessively. They worry about their health, and whether they will be able to get or keep a job, and thus be able to feed themselves and a family. Many people worry about events beyond their control that could adversely affect their lives. Fortunately, we can also use cognitive techniques to reduce worries.

I spent a great deal of my life worrying unnecessarily, a bad habit I continuously have to work with. As Martin Seligman writes in his book *Learned Optimism*, it is a scientific fact that there are optimists and pessimists, and that many more pessimists suffer from illnesses such as anxiety and depression than optimists. Our basic view of the world does not only affect our mental health; optimists rarely get physically sick, and they less frequently and to a lesser extent than the pessimists get common illnesses like colds and flu.

Of course, the placebo and nocebo effects, which I wrote about in the beginning, play an important role here. What we believe tends to become our reality, and that alone is a reason to work on moving from pessimism to optimism.

Note that there are not only downsides to being a pessimist. One advantage is that pessimists are rarely negatively surprised, because they often expect a negative outcome to begin with. There is probably also less chance of a pessimist being injured, because he or she is naturally more cautious and takes fewer chances.

Pessimism is a useful trait in quite a few professions. I want the engineers who constructed the bridge I drive on, or the plane

I am a passenger on, to have an inkling of pessimism, so that they have checked their numbers three or four times. The US space agency, NASA, uses this phenomenon deliberately in their recruitment. Since the *Challenger* accident, in which a space shuttle exploded just after launch, they are much more interested in pessimists when looking for new engineers and project managers.

Although there are benefits to pessimism, there is a clear disadvantage to unnecessary over-analyzing and worry. Worries tend to turn into overthinking, which can eventually become quite manic and repetitive, and even end up as damaging negative thought patterns, which in my book *Rise from Darkness,* I call *demons.*

Fortunately, there is a lot you can do to reduce your worries. One of the first things you can do is passively observe how you worry, when you worry, and what you worry about. Note this down in a diary or similar.

An even more effective technique is to write down what you worry about on small pieces of paper that you put in a box. At certain times, such as once or twice a year, you can bring out the notes and check how many of the concerns actually eventuated. You will see that very few of them happened. To illustrate this, you can put the notes in two piles: one for what actually happened, and the other for unnecessary concerns. Notice that the pile of the things you worried about that did not happen is much larger than the other.

TECHNIQUE: THE WORRY BOX

- Get yourself a stack of small sheets of paper and a box.
- Every time you worry about something, write your concern on one of the sheets of paper.
- Put the note in the box.

- Every 6 or 12 months, bring out the box and read all the notes.
- Sort the notes into two piles: one for things you worried about that actually happened, and one for the things that did not happen.
- Which pile is the largest?
- Also notice whether the consequences of the worries that actually did happen were greater or lesser than you thought they would be.

You can also use the *Extended ABC*, as described above, to reduce your concerns.

1. First, describe your concern as rationally and objectively as possible. What are you worried about? How likely do you think it is that what you fear will happen? What are the realistic effects and consequences of the incident? What other similar concerns do you have? What goes on for you when you think about this concern? What thoughts and feelings do you have?

2. Then try to analyze whether there are thought fallacies and irrational thinking involved. For example, you might ask yourself if there are other people who have reason to worry about the same thing. Do they approach the problem in a different way? Is it possible that you are exaggerating the likelihood of the negative event happening, and that you are exaggerating the consequences of the event for you? You can ask others how they would relate to your concerns, but be sure to ask someone who thinks a little differently than you, so you do not just end up reinforcing your own way of thinking.

3. The third step is to determine other ways you can think about this concern. What can you do to reduce the chances of the event you are worried about taking place? What can you do to reduce the consequences, if it actually takes place? What do you have power and control over, and what can you not control? To go from overthinking to action can be an effective way to reduce the power of a concern. If you have done what you can to reduce the chance of something negative happening and to reduce the consequences if it actually happens, you can relax a bit more.

When it comes to combating excessive worries, the Serenity Prayer is a very useful doctrine. You may want to print it out and put it up somewhere where you can read it often.

God, grant me the serenity to accept the things I cannot change,
Courage to change the things I can,
And wisdom to know the difference.

REINHOLD NIEBUHR

The Serenity Prayer is also very useful as a guideline for handling the adversities of life, and increasing your sense of achievement and mastery. We will focus on this further in Step 12.

Cognitive Behavioral Therapy now has a younger sibling, called Metacognitive Therapy (MCT). Whereas CBT focuses on changing automatic thought patterns that cause you harm, MCT focuses on avoiding rumination altogether. I think these two therapeutic tools work great in tandem. If you were going to a therapist specializing in MCT, he or she would instruct you to schedule your worrying, and thus learn how to avoid excessive worrying or other automatic rumination.

Technique: Scheduling time for worrying

- Instead of continually worrying and ruminating about your pain and concerns, schedule a specific time for this activity.

- Schedule this for some time into the near future, e.g. you are allowed to worry all you want at noon tomorrow.

- When thoughts of worries and things you are concerned about appear, simply tell yourself to delay them until noon tomorrow (or some alternative time slot).

- You may benefit from combining this with mindfulness and meditation (Step 13), as these methods will teach you how to control what you think about by actively directing your attention toward your breathing and consequently away from your rumination.

The Two-step Method for Habit Change

As mentioned, getting rid of depression is largely about changing the habits of what you do and how you think. A (good or bad) habit consists of a pattern of behavior, a pattern of thoughts, or both.

To change a habit, you must first define a new one and practice it a sufficient number of times until it sticks, while avoiding the old habit you want to move away from. The theory is simple, but how do you put it into practice?

In the book *The Power of Habit*, Charles Duhigg shows us that a habit consists of three parts: 1. A trigger, 2. The habit itself, and 3. A reward.

| Trigger | → | Habit | → | Reward |

Let me give you an example. For a large part of my life I have had a bad eating habit.

The Trigger: My blood sugar is low because I have not eaten proper food or because it is too long since I last ate. The Habit: I eat chocolate, often a big Snickers bar. The Reward: The reward center in my brain triggers a large dose of the neurotransmitter dopamine. The consequence is a sense of well-being (followed by self-loathing and shame).

What Duhigg found during his research for the book was that the easiest way to change a habit was to replace the *content* of the habit, linked to the same trigger and the same reward. In my case, I can get the same reward by drinking a glass of orange juice or eating fruit when my blood sugar is low. Both fruit and orange juice contain quite a lot of glucose (fruit sugar), but they also contain many nutrients that are good for us. Chocolate generally does not, except for very dark chocolate, which contains antioxidants and other beneficial phyto-chemicals.

In order to change a habit in this way, you must first analyze yourself and your own habits and actions. We touched on this relationship in Step 9 and we have worked on it in this chapter. You must first understand yourself and which (bad) habits work against you.

Let us use an example. You have noticed that you often resort to alcohol when your depression is extra-intense. The *Trigger* is that the depression intensifies, the *Habit* is to drink alcohol, and the *Reward* is the dopamine release that follows. You can replace the habit by going for a walk.

But how do you change the content of the habit? The problem with habits is that they are often automatic; the trigger automatically leads to the habit, which automatically results in the reward. We need something to stop the automation.

The Two-step Method is a simple and useful technique used to replace a bad habit. The point is to block the automation that usually takes you from trigger to habit. When you stop the automation, you can put in another habit, or a different thought, that is more favorable for you.

The first step in this method is to stop the thoughts, just as if you were pressing the emergency button on a machine. Such emergency buttons must be readily available if they are to be effective. To successfully stop unwanted automatic thought and behavior patterns, you must practice the technique by repeating it many times.

The first thing you need is something to block the automation with – an emergency button. It might be an internal alarm, such as the sound of a gong played internally in your mind, or an internal image of a flash that is triggered. It can be anything and can contain both sound and images. Think start signal, cannon shot, dynamite detonating.

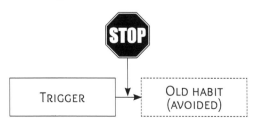

So if the habit is to eat chocolate when you are feeling depressed, you should let the alarm sound just as you are about to buy the chocolate.

Once you let the alarm sound, immediately replace the bad habit with one that is more appropriate. In order for this to work, you must have prepared the contents of the new habit in advance.

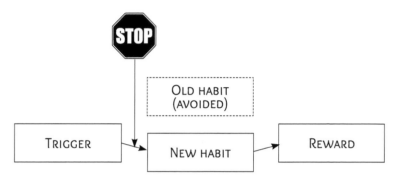

In the example with the chocolate, the new habit would be to buy and eat a piece of fruit or some fresh berries instead.

If the habit you want to change is about thoughts more than actions, you can replace the harmful thought with a mantra – a simple phrase you have created and practiced in advance.

Such a mantra could be:

It will be okay

Things will get better

Love yourself

I am good enough

Which mantra you use depends on the situation. For example, if you are beating yourself up, you can use the mantra *Love yourself*. You say it, even if you do not feel that you love yourself right there and then. The point is to stop the thoughts you do not want and replace them with better ones, and then it actually does not matter whether you wholeheartedly believe in the mantra or not. In Step 14 we will look at methods whereby you can increase your self-compassion and self-care.

When you use this technique to change your thinking, it looks like this:

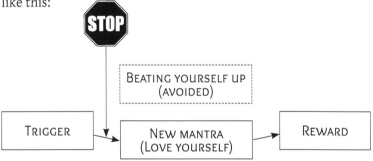

Technique: The Two-step Method for Habit Change

- Select a mental alarm. It could, for example, be the sound of a gong, a flash of light or a fire alarm. (Whatever you choose, "play" it inside your mind.)

- If you are going to change a behavior-oriented habit, prepare the contents of the new habit, such as eating fruit instead of chocolate. This means that you must be prepared and have bought the fruit in advance.

- If you are going to change an automatic thought pattern, prepare protective thoughts or mantras to replace the negative and hurtful thoughts you want to stop.

- When you experience a negative trigger, do the following two things, one right after the other:

1. Let your mental alarm go off, and then immediately:

2. Replace the current habit with the new habit, or the negative thoughts with your new mantra.

ZERO F*CKS GIVEN

There are several aspects of my life that are not ideal, such as the constant ringing in my ears, some other health problems and various concerns. Sometimes I simply need to not give a damn about the problems. Zero F*cks Given is therefore a habit I have incorporated and which I find very useful.

I use a variant of the Two-step Method to do this.

The tinnitus in my ears varies with the noise levels I am exposed to (the sound level of concerts, traffic noise and other sounds increases the tinnitus) and can reach quite disturbing levels. It is easy to respond to the sound with frustration and sometimes desperation. When that happens, I use the Two-step Method to stop the lingering of the pain.

First, I stop the negative train of thoughts, using the mental emergency button I described above. Then I add my mantra, which in this case is "Fuck it!" or "I don't give a shit!" It is vulgar, but it works really well for me, and that is the only thing that matters. It is my way of reminding myself that pain exists in everyone's life, including mine, but that I can ignore it and let it disappear by itself. Note that ignoring the pain is not the same as displacing it, but rather choosing not to pay attention to it and not to dwell on it. Acknowledge that it is there and choose to focus on something else.

A good combination when using this technique is to follow up with thinking about what you have in your life that you are grateful for. This way it becomes a kind of three-step technique: I stop the negative thinking, insert a useful mantra, and finish by thinking about something I am grateful for.

The Zero F*cks Given approach is not to be used for everything in life, as that would only lead to nihilism, the belief that nothing matters. But over time, you can learn when it is useful to not give a damn and when it is useful to focus on and increase the meaning of something. This is also part of learning to let go of the pain in life, and focus on that which you have reason to be grateful for. What you focus attention on is often the difference between depression and happiness.

TECHNIQUE: ZERO F*cks GIVEN

- When a negative train of thought appears, first use the Two-step Method to stop it, using a mental emergency button.
- Then insert a mantra like "I don't give a damn."
- Finally, focus your attention on something you are grateful for.

Chapter Summary

- In order to deal with the complexity of the world and to simplify our information processing, the brain creates a model based on different so-called schemata of the concepts in the world (one schema for the concept Human, another for the concept Dog, and so on).

- Schemata can be distorted and become unhealthy reality filters (convictions) that shape how you think and feel about events in your life. These reality filters often form the core of depression. The cure for depression is about changing these filters so that they do not produce negative thoughts and feelings.

- The way you change your reality filters is by becoming aware of what they contain and how they affect your thoughts and feelings. Then you can gradually repair them so they support you and no longer cause hurt and pain.

- Extended ABC is a simple and useful way to work with reality filters. This technique can also be used to reduce worries.

- To change a habit that is associated with either actions or thoughts, you can use the Two-step Method. It involves stopping automatic actions and thoughts that follow a negative trigger, and then inserting a more useful action or thought.

- An extension of the Two-step Method is to first stop a negative train of thought, not give a damn about the thing that bothers you, and then focus your attention on something you are grateful for.

Tasks This Week

☐ Take dietary supplements and eat at least a handful of vegetables every day.

☐ Go for a walk every day, or do some other form of aerobic exercise or movement that increases your heart rate.

☐ Keep a gratitude journal and add to it every evening.

☐ Practice *Extended ABC* every day.

Further Reading

Sarah Edelman: *Change Your Thinking*

Step 11:

CREATE MEANING IN YOUR LIFE

Many people who suffer from depression will at times experience life as quite meaningless. A lack of meaning and purpose in life can aggravate depression, and it is very useful to look at what you can do to increase the level of meaning.

History is full of people who have suffered from depression and other painful conditions and managed to stay on their feet and live a life worth living by finding meaning in it. For example, as a young man, American architect and inventor Buckminster Fuller was severely depressed and on the verge of suicide. He survived because he decided to devote his life to humanity by conducting research that would benefit the world. His autobiography, *Critical Path*, is an interesting read that says a lot about how you can make the world a better place and improve your own life in the process.

Another even stronger example is the Austrian psychologist Viktor E. Frankl, who was Jewish and taken to Auschwitz by the Nazis. Frankl experienced the horrors of the death camps and lost more or less everyone he loved, including his pregnant wife. It is almost impossible to imagine a worse fate than Frankl's.

He was academically interested in what separated those who survived the Holocaust from those who died. He arrived in Auschwitz with a manuscript for a book about meaning as a therapeutic tool. The manuscript was taken from him, but he developed his ideas of meaning further during his time in Auschwitz. What he saw was that those who had something to live for were much more likely to survive than those who did not, regardless of who initially was better physically equipped. As Friedrich Nietzsche wrote: *He who has a why to live can bear almost any how.*

Frankl developed this concept further and eventually called it *logotherapy*, which can be translated into something like *therapy through meaning.* He wrote several books on the subject, including *Man's Search for Meaning*, which he wrote in a few days after he was finally released from Auschwitz.

After the war, Frankl worked for several decades as a therapist in Vienna. One day, a new patient came into his clinic. It was an elderly gentleman who was severely depressed because he had lost his wife. Frankl asked him what it would be like for his wife to be left behind if he had been the one who died first. The older man replied that it would have ruined her life. Frankl then pointed out the suffering she had been spared. The man thought for a moment, stood up, shook Viktor Frankl's hand and left the room. He never returned; he had found an answer that gave him peace of mind. The fact that he had spared his wife from grief gave him meaning and purpose.

I had a similar experience. For many years, the one thing that kept me from taking my own life was the meaning I found in sparing my family from another death after my father had passed away. That view gave me enough fuel to get me through my worst years, until I could work on improving my condition.

But what if you feel that your life is completely without purpose and you have no idea how to find something that is meaningful to you?

According to Frankl, every human being will find meaning through one or more of the following: 1. To create something or perform a deed, 2. An experience or encounter with another human being (for example, to have a deep and meaningful love for someone), or 3. To find meaning in our response to suffering.

The story of the older gentleman, as well as my own story of sparing my mother and sister, are examples of the third point. However, I think we find the most common and important source of meaning in his first point; in a cause or creative work.

In the next chapter, we are going to look at how to write a mission statement. This is a personal formulation of how you want to use your life and can serve as a compass to point you to where you can find meaning.

I find it deeply meaningful to dedicate time to helping people who struggle with depression. Maybe you can help someone around you? If you do not know where to start, check with your church/religious congregation, or local charities that need volunteers. There are many activities you can do to help others: spending time with lonely, elderly people, homework support for children and adolescents, and much more.

Alternatively, you can find a cause to which you can devote time and energy. The environmental cause is desperate for more people. There are still millions of people in the world living below the poverty line. There is no shortage of good causes in the world, but there is a lack of volunteers.

There is a lot of research that tells us that doing something for others has a powerful positive effect on our mood. You can offer to walk your neighbor's dog, mow the lawn for your elderly uncle, or bake a cake for your local church. There is an endless list of good deeds waiting to be done. See what happens to your mood if you aim to do at least one good deed every day. It does not have to be anything big, just small everyday acts that make someone happy.

Once when I was in a miserable mood, I went to a convenience store in my hometown of Oslo and took out the equivalent of 20 dollars in small notes. Then I walked up and down the main street in search of homeless people. I gave the equivalent of a dollar or two to each of them.

A lot can be said about whether to give money to beggars or not, but I can tell you this: I left Karl Johan's street with a big smile on my face, and my good mood lasted all day and evening. It's probably the best 20 bucks I ever spent.

CHAPTER SUMMARY

- Even a broken life can be restored to a life worth living by adding purpose and meaning.

- Meaning can be found in human relationships, or by devoting yourself to a cause greater than yourself. It can also be found in your response to suffering; for example, when your suffering reduces others'.

- Even if you are not well, you can make a difference for others by, for example, getting involved with a local volunteering group.

 ## TASKS THIS WEEK

- ☐ Take dietary supplements and eat at least a handful of vegetables every day.

- ☐ Go for a walk every day, or do some other form of aerobic exercise or movement that increases your heart rate.

- ☐ Keep a gratitude journal and add to it every evening.

- ☐ Find something you can work with to give you a greater degree of meaning in life. Plan what you want to do with this.

 ## FURTHER READING

Viktor Frankl: *Man's Search for Meaning*

Step 12:

INCREASE YOUR SENSE OF ACHIEVEMENT

W hen your life has meaning, you can also increase your level of achievement, which is the theme of Step 12. Low self-esteem and lack of a sense of achievement are side effects of depression. It is difficult to have high self-esteem when you have a hyperactive inner critic in your head. It does not help when you have low energy levels, a low ability to concentrate or poor sleep either. Some people suffering from depression have a low ability to function in society, and that in itself is something that can aggravate the disease.

If you are a student with issues concentrating, you may get poor grades and a low attendance record. Maybe you have even given up altogether and dropped out of your course. If you are in the workforce, you may be struggling to keep a job or to get a job at all. Being unemployed can impact your self-confidence and sense of achievement.

As a result, the self-abuse and self-loathing increases, and you constantly give yourself a hard time, which leads to lower self-esteem. It is definitely a self-reinforcing downward spiral. Fortunately, it is possible to slow it down and eventually turn the spiral around.

As I mentioned in the introduction, the answer to poor self-esteem and little sense of achievement is to gradually build this up using low-level achievements. Set the bar as low as possible and avoid comparing yourself to others. Only you and your life are relevant here, because you are a unique individual. Gradually, scale up the level of ambition and complexity, step by step. When you do this, you also focus on resolving the various problems you may have in life; everything from health problems to financial struggles.

You can increase your sense of achievement both by working with achievement directly and by working to reduce and eventually get rid of depression in the long term. Here, we can again see that the different aspects of life affect each other and that it can be useful to work on more than one front at the same time. One example of this is how the increased physical exercise from Step 3 will lead to greater self-confidence, which again leads to an increased level of achievement. In this chapter, we will take a closer look at how you can directly increase your sense of achievement. But first, let's take a look at various practical problems you might have in your life, and how to resolve them.

Solve Problems in Your Life

As we've seen in the book so far, there are several sources of depression. One category of sources is that something has gone wrong in life; for example, issues connected to your financial situation. If your finances are a mess, you will need to resolve that situation in order to remove it as a source of further depression.

The same goes for other conflicts and problems, such as relational issues (which we looked at in Step 8), having lost a job or dropped out of school, having additional health problems (addressed in Steps 2, 3 and 5) or acquired a serious addiction to alcohol or drugs.

Life can be filled with all sorts of problems, and depending on the issue, they can be easily fixed, or very hard to rectify (and everything in between). I operate with a standard procedure for handling adversity and problems in life. It is heavily inspired by the Serenity Prayer from Step 10. It goes like this:

1. Get an overview of the situation.
2. Understand what you can change, and what you cannot change.
3. Take mitigative action where you can.
4. Seek help from others.
5. Accept that which you cannot change.

The first step in this process is to understand the situation you're in. If you have monetary problems, quantify them. What is the source of the money problems? Do you have debt? If so, how much? What is the interest rate of the debts that you carry? What is your level of income and expenses? When is payment of the debt and other expenses due?

Once you've completed an analysis of the situation, separate what you can change from what you cannot. If you have health problems, your illness might not be entirely curable (such as diabetes), but in most cases you can alleviate symptoms by following a healthier lifestyle (exercising more, eating healthier). You can reduce your suffering, even if you cannot remove the sickness altogether.

If you have relational problems, in most cases you can reduce conflict by confronting the people with whom you have difficulties, and discussing the problems with an open mind and a spirit of cooperation. In some cases, all the dialogue in the world cannot solve the underlying conflict, but in many cases you won't know what you can change and what you can't before you've tried!

When you've clearly identified the potential for resolving your problems, and distinguished it from those areas you simply cannot change, it's time to take mitigative action. Again, to use the example of monetary issues, call your debtors and seek to reduce the debt with a realistic down-payment plan. Consolidate small loans and credit card bills into one larger debt, which is likely to carry a lower interest rate.

When it comes to the gap between income and expenses, identify all your expenses, and eliminate those you can. Think about how you could increase your income, without jeopardizing your need for rest and recuperation.

If you're without a job, think about how you can get one. Even if it seems difficult, make a plan for how you can secure a job by taking steps to become more attractive in the job market. This could entail additional education or training, enrolling in an internship that will give you much needed work experience, or using your network to identify suitable job opportunities. You could even go online to find various freelance opportunities on platforms such as Upwork or Fiverr.

The way I see it, there is no problem or conflict so serious that there isn't some kind of workable solution, or at least something you can do to alleviate your situation. The trick is to follow the process, and getting a clear view of the objective situation and determining the potential for improvement. You can follow the detailed plan to increase your sense of achievement later in the chapter to identify which mitigative action is relevant to your situation.

The fourth step of the process is to seek help from others. In some countries, there are strong social security nets which will make this process easier. In others, like the US, this is not always the case. In such cases, seeking help from friends and family will be even more important. If your friends and family are unwilling or unable to offer help, seek out your local church or congregation. Most people will appreciate being asked to help, as long as they are in a situation where they are able to do so.

The final step of this process is to accept that which you cannot change. Go back to Step 1 and read about acceptance. Accepting that life took turns you didn't expect or didn't want can take time. But in the end, the choice often stands between acceptance and continued suffering. You are fighting for the quality of the rest of your life, and accepting adversity and trauma you can do nothing about is often a very important step toward recovery and improvement. Time will work for you, and make it easier to find acceptance.

FIND YOUR STRONG SUITS AND BUILD YOUR LIFE AROUND THEM

When the goal is to achieve more, one very important principle is to be true to yourself. Let us say you completed your education because it made sense, or because your parents put pressure on you to take that particular path. Over time, a serious imbalance between what you *do* and who you really *are* can build up. Such an imbalance can contribute to depression because you spend your time on something you do not really want to do.

If you are an established adult when you discover such an imbalance, it is, fortunately, not necessary to quit your job in order to restore it. You can have a job that gives you an income you can live off, whilst cultivating hobbies and interests in your spare time. Your job does not have to be the main arena in which you realize yourself.

Someone I know found another way to restore the imbalance. She quit her job as a lawyer because she had a strong drive toward visual art. Now she teaches law and spends the rest of her time painting.

But what if you do not know yourself enough to know what you really want? For younger people, this is probably the rule rather than the exception. The world is so full of opportunities and choices that you might almost miss the old days, when it was natural to follow in your parents' footsteps.

My own solution is to go on an annual camping trip in the forest, alone. I usually find the answers I am looking for there, in the silence of the forest.

You don't have to go exploring in the forest to find yours. There are several things you can do to find out who you are. You can map out your key strengths; within positive psychology these are called *signature strengths*. You may think *I do not have any strengths; I am not good at anything.* Do not worry if this is how you think, because it is just a lie, and I am about to prove it to you.

Everyone has signature strengths. These are the good traits you have, both those that naturally make up a central part of your personality, and the traits you have learned by practicing over time. For example, a good accountant is likely to have *accuracy* as a core strength, while a nurse has *caring* as one of theirs.

The easiest way to get clear on your strengths is to use the free online form at viacharacter.org, developed by researchers working within positive psychology. I encourage you to use this as it will help you find out what your strengths are.

You can also find a mentor – an older person who can advise you on which paths to take. If you do not know anyone who can do this for free, spend some money and go and talk to an experienced and skilled life coach or career counsellor.

Over time, you can reflect on the changes you can make to live more in line with your own strengths and who you really *are*. This not only applies to your education and career choices, but also what you do in your spare time. By getting to know yourself better in this way and adjusting toward your own strengths, you have a good chance of gaining a sense of self-trust, achievement and satisfaction with yourself and your life. It will give you an enhanced sense of meaning when you live aligned with your true self.

A Detailed Plan to Increase Your Sense of Achievement

The following is a concrete plan to increase your sense of achievement. This is relevant both to solving negative problems, and to achieve positive things you can be proud of.

1. Write a Mission Statement

A mission statement is a written statement of what you want to do with your life. I can imagine you might be frowning a bit right now. You may think that you have more than enough to do, dealing with a difficult illness. But, as we discussed in the previous chapter, having meaning in your life will make it much easier to deal with the difficult and painful sides. A mission statement will raise your awareness about how you really want to spend your life, even if you suffer right now.

Hopefully you got some ideas while reading the previous chapter. Maybe you are already embarking on a career that is aligned with what you care about the most. Maybe you are confused. Maybe you have no idea what to write in a mission statement. If that is the case, I have written a relatively general statement below that you can use to get started when writing your own. You can even copy it and use it as inspiration until you find out more about what you want.

I want to spend my life helping others. I will seek and find people that I can help by being present with them, listening to them, and helping them with practical tasks. I have a unique position and experience that makes it possible for me to contribute, because I have known hard times in my life. I am now on a path that will gradually lead me to a better life, with an increased degree of positive emotions and more meaning.

Whether you copy the above or write your own, make sure to take your strengths into account. These signature strengths can provide basic information about what kind of life direction you will be most satisfied with.

A mission statement should be a living document. Life changes as you live it, and it may be necessary to update the mission statement from time to time. I update mine several times a year, usually after the camping trip I mentioned. When you understand that you always have the option to change your mission statement, it will also be easier to write your first version.

2. Derive a Set of Major Strategic Goals from Your Mission Statement

Major strategic goals are big, important goals, which will take months to years to achieve. When you suffer from depression, your main goal might look something like this:

> *I will recover from depression, or at least live a much better life. I will have made significant progress within five years.*

Other major strategic goals can be deduced from the mission statement above. Such as:

> *Within two years, at least one person has told me that the help I gave them was significant.*

This was the main strategic goal I had when I wrote my book *Rise from Darkness*. I told myself that if only one person told me that the book made a difference to them, my mission would be accomplished. So far, I have received this feedback from hundreds of people. I have no words for how important and meaningful this is to me; this is really one of the most important things in my life.

Here are other examples of major strategic goals:

> *I complete a half marathon within two years.*
> *I have gained control of my addiction within five years.*
> *I have lost 10 kg (22 pounds) of weight within a year.*
> *I am employed in a job that I enjoy within two years.*

Write down your strategic goals in a notebook or in a digital format. Make sure to note the date when you defined the goal. You will see that when you follow this method, there is almost no limit to the number of positive things that can happen.

3. Derive a Set of Sub-goals from Your Major Strategic Goals

What we are doing here is dividing big, strategic goals (like getting rid of depression) into smaller, manageable sub-goals. Let us take the half marathon goal above as an example.

Strategic goal: *I complete a half marathon within two years.*
Sub-goals:

1. 0-2 months: I start by taking a walk every day.

2. 2-6 months: In addition to the daily walks, I run 2-3 times a week. I start with very short runs and gradually increase the distance to 4 km (2.5 mi).

3. 6-18 months: I run 3 times a week, gradually increasing the distance to 10 km (6.2 mi).

4. 18-24 months: I follow a half marathon training program, which I found online.

Here is another example:

Strategic goal: *I am employed in a job that I enjoy within two years.*
Sub-goals:

1. I think through and identify what types of jobs I think I will enjoy.

2. I find out what I need to be able to do in order to get such a job (courses, further education, on-the-job training, etc.).

3. I do what I need to do in terms of extra training or courses.

4. I use my network to find out which companies or organizations offer these types of jobs.

5. I contact the appropriate organizations and ask for an open interview.

6. Because I am prepared and I have the skills the job requires, I get the job.

DERIVE SPECIFIC TASKS FROM THE SUB-GOALS AND CREATE A PRIORITIZED TO-DO LIST

We have gone from a mission statement to major strategic goals to sub-goals, and now we are getting to the lowest level in this hierarchy, which is looking at specific tasks.

If you have a list of sub-goals as in both of the examples above, you simply take the first sub-goal and derive a set of specific tasks using the sub-goal as a starting point. Ask yourself: If I am to reach this sub-goal, what specifically do I have to *do*?

If we use the goal of getting a job you like as an example, specific tasks for the first sub-goal could be:

- Talk to people who know me, and ask them what work they think I would be suitable for.
- Talk to a career advisor.
- Take a couple of personality tests to find out what I am good at.
- Talk to my supervisor at my school or university.
- Talk to my uncle, who works within HR and recruitment, and ask him for advice.

Here you have a to-do list, which you can use as a starting point as you keep working. This is where I get to the last point: List your tasks in order of priority. This way the list will become much more efficient. Ask yourself the question: What is the most important thing I can do today to move toward my sub-goal, and eventually the major goal? What can I do now that will make the other tasks unnecessary or easier?

Then you give that task a go. Then the next. Before you know it, you'll have got what you want!

Note that the procedure with strategies and a to-do list will make it easier for you to perform the techniques and take the measures I recommend in this book. I routinely use this procedure several times each week, and I would highly recommend you start practicing this habit. Do not worry about not getting it right in the beginning, just keep using it and you will see that it gradually sets in as a habit that you will greatly benefit from.

TECHNIQUE: PROCEDURE FOR INCREASED SENSE OF ACHIEVEMENT

1. Write a mission statement, stating what you want to focus on in life.
2. Derive one or more major strategic goals from your mission statement.
3. Derive sub-goals from your major strategic goal(s).
4. Derive specific tasks from your sub-goals.
5. Make a prioritized to-do list.
6. Hit the first and most important task.
7. Follow the prioritized to-do list.

Chapter Summary

- Many people with depression experience a lack of self-confidence and sense of achievement, and it is important to improve this. The feeling that you are achieving things in your life supports a sound and healthy mind.

- You increase your sense of achievement by succeeding more at what is important to you, and you do this by setting goals that are easy to achieve in the beginning, and then gradually increasing ambition and complexity over time.

- The standard process for solving problems in life consists of the following five steps: 1. Get an overview of the situation, 2. Understand what you can change, and what you cannot change, 3. Take mitigative action where you can, 4. Seek help from others, and 5. Accept that which you cannot change.

- Build your life around your signature strengths, which will help increase your sense of achievement.

- Use the procedure for increased sense of achievement to build self-confidence and life satisfaction.

Tasks This Week

- [ ] Take dietary supplements and eat at least a handful of vegetables every day.

- [ ] Go for a walk every day, or do some other form of aerobic exercise or movement that increases your heart rate.

- [ ] Keep a gratitude journal and add to it every evening.

- [ ] Choose one problem in your life, and make a plan to resolve it using the standard method to solve it above.

- [ ] Take the test on viacharacter.org to determine your signature strengths.

- [ ] Plan how to increase your sense of achievement in your life.

 ## Further Reading

Stephen R. Covey: *The 7 Habits of Highly Effective People*

Step 13:

LEARN MEDITATION, MINDFULNESS AND SELF-HYPNOSIS

In Step 13, we will look at several techniques that can be extremely effective in reducing depression and other mental illnesses: meditation, mindfulness, and self-hypnosis. I believe that these techniques, along with Steps 3, 7 and 10, are the most central parts of this program.

The more I read about and practice meditation, the more convinced I become that it is an effective tool in creating a better life. There is a vast array of research showing that meditation lowers blood pressure, lowers resting heart rate, increases willpower and reduces stress. Meditation allows the body's nervous system to reset, restoring the balance of hormones and neurotransmitters. Since these substances to a large extent constitute your emotions, meditation has a direct positive effect on your mood.

Meditation, mindfulness and self-hypnosis are techniques that are related to each other. They all shift the brain's operating mode to a level that allows for repair, learning and maintenance. In this way, they somewhat have the same function as sleep. We can say that the brain has several gears, much like a bicycle. By this I mean the electrochemical activity of the nerve cells operates like brain waves, which appear at different speeds. These waves can be measured using electrodes placed on the skull. The brain has been found to operate within the following frequency ranges: Delta, Theta, Alpha and Beta.

Delta brainwaves are used for the brain activity level we have when we are in deep sleep. Delta equals 0.5-3 cycles per second, also called hertz (in physics written as Hz).

The Theta range equals 4-7 hertz and is the brain activity level we have when we are in a light sleep. This brain activity level is associated with high activity in the subconscious mind, and you are often on this level when you dream or daydream. It is also possible to reach this level in an awakened state, through meditation and self-hypnosis.

In the Alpha range, the brain operates at 8-12 hertz. This brain activity level is referred to as relaxed concentration and is ideal for learning and tasks that require focus. The Alpha level is associated with creativity, imagination and inspiration, and enables long-term storage of information in the brain.

The Beta level is what many of us operate in daily, especially when life is hectic and we are stressed. When your head is racing, your brain is operating in the Beta level. The more stressed you are, the higher speed your brain operates at. Beta brain waves range between 13-36 hertz.

It is healthy to regularly get the brain into a lower gear and achieve a greater degree of Alpha rather than Beta. This is exactly what you can do through meditation, mindfulness and self-hypnosis.

Although there are many similarities between the three methods mentioned, I will treat them separately. Later, I will give you some specific techniques you can start practicing straight away, to take advantage of some of the health benefits.

MEDITATION

Meditation is the art of quieting the mind through various techniques to focus the attention, often on your breath. There are many different meditation techniques, and they usually have certain features in common. They are exercises to remove the daily hustle and bustle of thoughts and focus on a single mantra, or just on the breath. The essence of most meditation techniques is to focus on the breath to calm the mind. Breathing deeply and calmly is healthy and useful on its own. When you breathe this way, your body reduces the level of stress hormones such as adrenaline and cortisol. In fact, breathing deeply and calmly also works as pain relief, due to the endorphin production that comes with it.

An important trick in meditation is that it doesn't work to try and force the intruding thoughts away. What works is to actively revert your attention back to your breath. In other words, it's easier to divert your attention *toward* something than *away* from something. This is an important point.

The mind can only contain one primary thought at a time, and by actively choosing that thought, you are at the same time choosing not to focus on worries and other automatic, negative thought patterns. Thus, you give yourself a pause from all those painful thoughts while you meditate. Since your pain originates from focusing your attention on historic trauma, negative self-chatter, worries and other negative trains of thought, a key skill to reduce that pain is to learn how to direct your attention toward something more positive. This is what you learn when practicing meditation. It is also what we practiced in Step 7, albeit with different methods.

Below is a simple meditation method you can try right now.

SIMPLE MEDITATION

Lie on a sofa or bed or sit in a comfortable chair. Wear loose and comfortable clothing. Turn the phone to silent or turn it off completely. Turn off other audio sources.

Try to relax as best you can. Then count to ten. Concentrate fully on the count and try to avoid being distracted, simply by reverting to the counting. Once you have counted to ten, do it again. Repeatedly count to ten. As you count, you will notice that thoughts are creeping in – concerns, plans, and various other thoughts. This is to be expected. When a thought appears, just let it go and bring your attention back to the count. Continue the count for five to ten minutes.

Congratulations! You have just meditated for the first time. It was quite easy, right? Now, let us take it a step further, with a slightly more advanced method.

As you sit or lie down, allow your attention to pass through your body. Notice if it hurts anywhere, if you have any sore or tight muscles. Then let your attention go to your surroundings. What sounds do you hear? Are there any smells where you are? What does the environment look like, what colors do you see? What kind of texture does the wall have, the ceiling, the floor?

Then turn your attention back to yourself. You can close your eyes if you want to, but it is not necessary.

Focus your attention on your breath. Is it smooth? How fast is it going? How deeply are you breathing? Place one hand on your belly as you breathe. Can you feel your belly expand when you inhale and release when you exhale? Try to breathe so you feel it in your belly. This is healthy, deep breathing, and you will gradually become better at it.

As you breathe, try slowing down the speed (frequency) of your breath. See how slowly you can breathe without feeling that you lack oxygen. Let your breath be natural as you gradually slow it down. Notice if your breath is smooth and even as you breath in and out, or if it becomes a bit choppy. The latter is quite common, especially when people are stressed. Many people are not used to breathing deeply and evenly.

After a good number of deep breaths in and out, start counting. Slowly count to four as you inhale. Then do the same while exhaling. Breathe at a pace that feels natural and comfortable.

Continue to relax as you count to four on each inhale and each exhale. Thoughts will definitely pop up as you keep going. Once again, just let them go, like clouds in a blue sky on a windy day, and take your attention back to your breath. This is the core of the technique: allowing thoughts to pass on their own, while quietly guiding your attention back to your breath.

After practicing this breathing method for 10-15 minutes, you can finish the meditation.

You can meditate like this every day and gradually increase your time to 30-45 minutes. If you meditate in the evening, you may well fall asleep. If you usually struggle to go to sleep, it's an added benefit that the meditation makes you sleepy, although it will cut into your meditation time. If you want to avoid falling asleep when meditating, you can meditate in the middle of the day or in the morning. It does not matter when you meditate; just that you actually do.

THE BODY SCAN

After a week of the simple meditation technique I described above, you are ready to take it another step further, using a technique called the Body Scan. Here you "scan" the body, part by part.

Lie down and breathe calmly for a few minutes, counting to four on your inhales and exhales. Then go through your body, body part by body part, and let go of each one of them. Start with the left foot. Inhale while counting to four, exhale while counting to four. On the exhale, imagine that you let go of the foot, and allow it to go its own way. You may wonder what I mean by letting go of a body part, but with practice you will understand the phrase. You will notice that letting go of the body part feels right and is comfortable.

After the left foot, do the same with the left ankle. Then the left leg, knee, thigh and hip. Then the parts of the right leg, in the same order. Then it is the arms' turn. Start with the left hand, then the left wrist, forearm, elbow, upper arm and finally the shoulder. Then do the same with your right arm. Continue by going over the different parts of your upper body. Begin with your pelvis, moving up along the front of the upper body: the abdominal area, the heart area and the lungs, the chest muscles, the neck. Then the back of the upper body: the buttocks, lower back, middle part of the back and shoulder blades, before ending with the neck. Last, you go through the different parts of the head: the face, the back of the head and finally the top of the head.

If you get lost, or forget which body part you were working on, you can either start again or with any part of the body. It does not matter if you forget a body part or two; the point of the exercise is just to go through your body, part by part, and achieve relaxation in your body and mind.

An alternative to mentally "letting go" of each body part is to pretend to breathe with it. You go through the body in the same way as described and in the same order. But for every body part you dwell on, you pretend to breathe in and out of that body part instead. It feels a bit strange the first few times, but after a while you will notice that it has the same effect as letting go.

You can choose one of the two above methods or alternate between them. Ideally, you have now started a lifelong habit – meditating several times a week – so it is important that you find a technique you like.

Personally, I find meditation comfortable, soothing, relaxing, soporific and healthy. I tend to meditate more when I feel stressed, as otherwise stress often leaves me with sore or tense muscles. I also actively use meditation as a way to get to sleep.

TECHNIQUE: BODY SCANNING

- Make sure you do your Body Scan at a time and place you are not going to be interrupted.
- Turn off your phone and put it away.
- Turn off music, TV and other appliances that make noises.
- Dim the lights to an appropriate level.

- Wear loose, comfortable clothing.
- Lie in a comfortable position on a bed or other soft surface.
- Breathe in and out slowly a few times, counting to four on each inhale and to four on each exhale.
- Option 1: Go through your entire body and focus for a moment on each body part. As you focus on each body part, imagine that you are releasing control of that body part and that you let it go its own way.
- Option 2: Instead of letting go of each body part, imagine breathing in and out of that body part.
- Whether you do option 1 or 2, start with your left leg. Go through your leg in this order: foot, ankle, leg, knee, thigh, hip.
- Then go through your right leg in the same way.
- Then there is your left arm; follow this order: hand, wrist, forearm, elbow, upper arm, shoulder.
- Do the same with your right arm.
- Then go through your upper body: your pelvis, abdominal region, heart region, lungs, chest muscles, neck, buttocks, lower back, middle part of your back, shoulder blades, neck.
- Finally, the head, in this order: your face, the back of your head and the top of your head.

If you find it difficult to read instructions while meditating, you can use an audio recording of a guided meditation. I have shared a recording which you can find under *Resources* on kristianhall. com. You can also find it by searching for "Kristian Hall meditation" on YouTube. Alternatively, there are several meditation apps, such as Calm and Headspace, which you can download to your phone.

Mindfulness

Many people go through life more or less continually stressed. Endless chores, plans, and worries haunt the brain like nightmares. Mindfulness means that you stop this flow of thoughts, take a break and just exist in the here and now, without judging the experience.

Imagine that you are sitting on a bus, looking out of the window. You just take in the surroundings outside the bus, without even thinking about it. You are fully present there and then, without judging or analyzing what is going on. This experience is mindfulness.

In summary, we can say that mindfulness is the Western world's interpretation of the ancient Oriental spiritual principles. The roots of mindfulness are found in Buddhism and Hinduism. In particular, one branch of Buddhism, called Zen Buddhism, has been a fundamental inspiration for mindfulness. Mindfulness means an aim to be present here and now as much as possible. It is a state many of us do not reach often, especially when we are depressed.

American doctor Jon Kabat-Zinn has been credited with being one of the most important contributors in bringing the Eastern disciplines that form the basis of mindfulness into the Western world. Throughout his career, he has worked on designing and promoting programs on how to use mindfulness to reduce stress, anxiety and depression. Amongst other things, he is one of the people behind the *Mindfulness Based Stress Reduction* (MBSR) program, which is largely about practicing meditation for 12 weeks (with guidance once a week). Participants are encouraged to meditate for 45 minutes every day for 12 weeks. I highly recommend the book *Full Catastrophe Living*, which includes a complete course of this program.

Through various techniques, we can increase the time in which we are fully present and considerably reduce our stress levels. This way, we achieve many significant health benefits. *Full Catastrophe Living* illustrate this very well. Kabat-Zinn describes how patients who the health care system has given up on often come to his clinic. They arrive with severe chronic pain, deep anxiety and depression, and when they leave the program they are transformed. Of course, not everyone who completes a mindfulness course gets their life turned around, but it has been the saving grace for many.

When you practice mindfulness, you get a break from the painful feelings and thoughts, because most of the pain is associated with either the future or the past. Grief, for example, is associated with both the past and the future, while worry is associated with the future. If you manage to live in the here and now, at this very moment, there is *no room for pain*. It is a magical feeling when you experience it for the first time.

A key concept within mindfulness is acceptance. In the end of the day, there are no bad and no good moments, there are only moments. Kabat-Zinn talks about how they use the phrase *rolling out the red carpet* to train patients in dealing with pain. Instead of panicking and trying to escape the pain, they are gradually trained to confront it, accept it, and make it a part of themselves.

From my own experience, I know that this works. As mentioned, I have chronic tinnitus due to noise from machine guns and tanks from my time in the military. I will never experience complete silence in my life. There is no doubt that this problem added to my depression. In order to get better, I had to accept the sounds, make them a part of myself.

The turning point for me was when one of my friends, a wise person who later became a psychologist, said: *Why not just think: "what a cool sound"?* I can assure you that I found this very provoking at the time! But then I thought about what he had said and decided to give it a try. Although it was impossible to see the sounds as something positive, I chose to explore them, uncover the different layers of them, and count the many different parts they consisted of. In this way I managed to make the sounds a part of my reality. Because they are. I stopped trying to escape from them. This has led me to be able to live with them without it bringing me down.

You can do the same with your depression and painful feelings. Accept them as something that is here and now, without judgement. Try to think that at least your painful feelings are known feelings. They are terrible to be in the middle of, but they are familiar territory. Try to cultivate feelings of pride and self-respect from the fact that you are able to remain standing in a storm of emotions that would bring many others down (because you have experience with these feelings, which others have not).

But never worship your depression. Do not make it a part of your identity. I see too many people, especially young people, doing exactly this. They put their depression on a pedestal, worship it, marinate themselves in it. I did it myself. But it does not lead anywhere good, only further down. Instead, you can accept the feelings for what they are and tell yourself that you can endure them and that you will gradually let go of them. For you are in the process of achieving exactly that!

SELF-HYPNOSIS

Of the three methods you can use to increase relaxation and reduce brain speed, self-hypnosis is probably my favorite. There are several reasons for this and the most important is that with self-hypnosis you can add automated improvement elements, a way to reprogram the brain that leads to a better life in almost any area you want.

Self-hypnosis is a form of targeted meditation. While it has similar effects on the body and mind as meditation, it also allows for a profound change of the mind. Self-hypnosis can be used to stop smoking, to fall asleep or to reduce depression, which is of course the main purpose here. It is actually very simple. Make an audio recording with the desired text, lie down or sit in a comfortable position and press "Play." Just as with meditation, it is important to make sure that you are not going to be disturbed while listening to the recording. Put the phone on silent or turn it off, and turn off all other audio sources. Then listen attentively to the recording.

The most time and effort required when using self-hypnosis is in writing the contents of the hypnosis recording (a so-called script), and recording it on a suitable platform. But here comes the good news – I've already done this for you, so you can start your self-hypnosis right away.

You have two options. The quickest way is to go to kristian-hall.com and click on *Resources,* or to search for "Kristian Hall self-hypnosis" on YouTube. There you will find a ready-made recording for you to listen to.

The other option is to record your own version of the script. The advantage of doing this is that you can adjust the script and add things that are more relevant to you and your situation. If you never have tried self-hypnosis before, I recommend you start with my pre-recorded audio. If you find it effective, then you can go ahead and write and record your own scripts.

Let us take a closer look at how and why self-hypnosis works. Have a look at some of the negative messages you tell yourself. Where did they come from? Perhaps they are not yours at all, but rather originated from your parents or someone who bullied you. Statements like:

> *I can't do anything right*
> *I'm a bad person*
> *I can't play music or sing*
> *I'm terrible at sports*
> *I'm not funny*
> *I don't deserve ... (Insert something you think you do not deserve)*

Unfortunately, parents say things like, "You don't deserve this," or "You can't do anything right," or "You're a bad boy/ girl." When this is said repeatedly during a vulnerable time of our development, especially in our early childhood, it leaves scars. These scars become trapped in your brain and subconsciously affect you more or less constantly. This causes you to continuously give yourself a hard time.

If you have been bullied, it will have the same effect. After hearing others give you a hard time, you gradually take over the "responsibility" and start giving yourself a hard time too.

The bottom line is that these statements, whether they are your own or come from others, is a form of self-hypnosis. When you go through your day telling yourself *I'm not worthy of anything, I never succeed at anything, no one will ever love me*, this is continuous self-hypnosis. You will begin to listen to your voice and accept what it is telling you. It will become your reality. You say: *No one will ever love me*, and not only do you believe it, but you actually stop loving yourself.

Fortunately, this phenomenon also works in the other direction. Through your own custom-written script and targeted self-hypnosis, you can turn your negative thoughts about yourself into positive ones. For example, you could include sentences like the ones below in your script:

> *There is a myriad of factories in your brain and in your body. They are capable of manufacturing the perfect mix of signal substances that you need to be a lot happier and to feel completely safe in all situations. You know it, deep down. You realize that your own body is capable of producing the substances that make you happy, much happier than you have ever been before. You notice how these factories listen to your voice and they have already started to produce the signal substances you need the most. You realize that you are well on your way to a brighter mind and a happier life.*

When you listen to a text like this while in a state of trance, you are very receptive to creating changes in your brain. What you are actually doing is re-writing some of the core programs in your brain in such a way that you achieve effective and profound changes.

If you think this method sounds a little scary, think about how much worse your depression is. If you're still cautious about trying this, start slowly with a script you trust. The script I have recorded, which you can find at kristianhall.com, is specifically written with this in mind. If you listen to it, you will notice that it only contains positive elements.

You need two things to succeed with your self-hypnosis: attention and repetition.

Attention means listening to the recording with as much focus as possible. Try to capture every word. Concentrating deeply on an external sound like this will automatically take you into a trance, which is the very same state you are in when you daydream. Being in a trance is by no means dangerous or harmful; it is about slowing down the speed of the brain and increasing the degree of focused attention.

Repetition means that it is not enough to listen to the recording every now and then. In my own experience, I need to listen to a recording every day for two weeks before I start to notice the effects. I am talking about profound positive effects. Self-hypnosis written for sleep works faster, simply because it tones down the part of the brain that worries and plays your automatic thought patterns. But it requires more time to achieve a profound change of habit. Therefore, do not give up on the self-hypnosis until you have tried it for some time.

Here are a few basic things to keep in mind when writing your own scripts: First of all, you should avoid writing about what you want to get *away from*. If you use words like grief, anxiety and depression in your script, you will inevitably activate the neural connections associated with those concepts. This means that you force the brain to think about the bad things. As we have seen, every time we think about the things that are painful, we produce signal substances associated with painful feelings. It is easy to avoid: Write about what you want to achieve instead. Instead of writing about anxiety, write about safety and calm. Instead of writing about depression, write about happiness and contentment. As you listen you will realize why, and that this is the point of the exercise. By only writing about positive situations, we train the brain to build new neural connections that are associated with positive concepts, which in turn triggers the production of signal substances associated with positive emotions.

Another important thing when writing your own scripts is that a script is similar to a computer program or legal contract in the sense that it is read and understood literally. It is like the story of Aladdin and the magic lamp. Be careful what you wish for. For example, if you write: *Your sleep is getting longer and longer every night*, you may find yourself actually sleeping longer and longer every night. This is not what you want. You want your sleep to be optimal, not last as long as possible. But do not be afraid to make mistakes; you'll quickly realize if you've written something that does not work. You can also contact a professional hypnotist and ask him or her to check the quality of your script.

TECHNIQUE: SELF-HYPNOSIS

- You can find a pre-recorded self-hypnosis recording under *Resources* at kristianhall.com.
- You can also create your own recording, using the recording feature on your mobile phone, or similar. If you go for this solution, first write down what you want to record (a so-called script).
- Sit in a comfortable chair or lie on a soft surface.

- Make sure you will not be disturbed during the self-hypnosis session. Put your phone on flight mode so no one can call you.
- Play the recording and listen to it carefully.

 CHAPTER SUMMARY

- There are many different types of meditation. Self-hypnosis is a kind of meditation.

- Meditation and self-hypnosis can be powerful tools to improve your life.

- Meditation is easy but requires continuous effort over a long period of time for it to work.

- Mindfulness has helped many people with depression, anxiety and other disorders. Find a course near you where you can learn the techniques.

- Self-hypnosis is easy to practice. All you need is a proper self-hypnosis recording (you can find an example at kristianhall.com) and time when you can focus and listen to it. Self-hypnosis requires a bit of repetition to be effective. After a few weeks, you may begin to notice the effects.

Tasks This Week

- [ ] Take dietary supplements and eat at least a handful of vegetables every day.

- [ ] Go for a walk every day, or do some other form of aerobic exercise or movement that increases your heart rate.

- [ ] Keep a gratitude journal and add to it every evening.

- [ ] Meditate every evening by doing the Body Scan (page 190). Alternative: Listen to the self-hypnosis recording every evening.

 ## Further Reading

Jon Kabat-Zinn: *Full Catastrophe Living*

Adam Eason: *The Secrets of Self-Hypnosis: Harnessing the Power of Your Unconscious Mind*

Step 14:

LEARN TO LOVE YOURSELF

N ow you have reached the very last step of the program. I am proud of you! In this step, we are going to look at how you can increase your levels of self-acceptance and self-care.

Depression is, as mentioned, largely about seeing everything through a set of filters. You look negatively at yourself, your surroundings, your world and your life. Many despise or hate themselves and they are rarely able to notice what is good in life, and what is good in themselves, because they are busy seeing everything as dark, gloomy, sad, and cruel. Little wonder they stay depressed.

An important key to recovery is eliminating these filters. Many of the techniques we have already worked on do exactly that, especially the gratitude part and the cognitive techniques. Over time, if you manage to work through these dimensions, you will certainly feel better and your life will start to brighten up.

Another way to remove the filters is to increase the degree of love and compassion you feel for yourself, your surroundings and the world. This is not done overnight, but can be achieved gradually through various techniques, including a special form of meditation I call the *Love Meditation*. I know it is a pompous name, but think about it: If you could exchange contempt for love, would you not be much better off? If you could love yourself, every day, and direct the same emotions toward those around you and the rest of the world, would it not be hard to stay depressed? Put the book aside for a moment and think about this. Allow yourself to let love in for a moment.

If you find it difficult, think back through your life and find a memory where you were genuinely happy, where you felt love. A tip: It is easier to find a memory of love for animals than for humans, because relationships with animals are so much less complicated. Do not worry if you are unable to find such a memory, but let it come to you at a later time. Everyone has a few memories like this, but sometimes it takes some time before they surface.

Once you arrive at your memory, allow yourself to "bathe" in it. Close your eyes, add some sounds, colors and movements to your memory so you can watch it as a movie, with your eyes being the camera. Add some nice music. Then run through this memory over and over again.

It lifted your mood a little, did it not? An exercise like this takes practice, and it may not work for you the first time, but repeating it can be a powerful technique to get an instant *mood boost*.

TECHNIQUE: BATHE IN GOOD MEMORIES

- It is a good idea to do a Body Scan before proceeding with this technique, to put yourself in the right mode.
- Choose a memory from your life that is purely positive, or as positive as possible.
- Relive the memory by slowly running it through your consciousness like a movie, as if you were sitting in a movie

theatre and the memory was being displayed on the screen with you as the camera. (Run through the memory from a first-person perspective.)

- Add colors, music and sounds to your memory.
- Run through the memory several times in the same session, until you notice an improvement in your mood.

In the book *Love Yourself Like Your Life Depends on It*, Kamal Ravikant talks about how he got rid of his depression by standing in front of the mirror every morning and repeatedly saying to himself: *I love you*. That was his recipe for getting well. Personally, I think it makes sense to add some additional mitigative action (the steps you find in this book), but gradually learning to love yourself is very important. It is something that will take time, because many depressions are based on self-loathing and self-hatred. But you can be happy with yourself again, because you were there once.

We are now going to go through a specific method of meditation for you to be happier and gain more respect for yourself and others, namely the Love Meditation.

Start the meditation the same way as you started the Body Scan. That is, lie down on a bed or other soft surface and make sure you are not going to be disturbed. Then slowly breathe in and out while you count to four on both the inhale and the exhale. Do a complete Body Scan before moving on to the love part. Through meditation, you reduce the level of stress hormones and other signaling substances associated with negative emotions and stress, and you increase the levels of signaling substances associated with relaxation and positive feelings. You will then be more receptive to the increased content of love that we will now introduce.

Once you have completed the Body Scan, lie still and breathe for a while. Then focus your attention on something or someone you love. Preferably a person you love and with whom you have no conflicts or negative feelings toward. A sister or brother you love and who loves you back is perfect; it does not have to be more complicated than that. As you picture this person, put a golden aura, a halo, around the person, as you say to yourself in your head: *I love you* (alternatively *I like you* or *I accept you*). Direct a wave of love toward the person as you say it. You can use animals too; pets are perfect. It might even be easier to feel pure, uncomplicated love for animals than for humans.

Repeat the same thing with other people you love. Picture them in front of you, put a golden aura around them and say: *I love you* (or use the options above), while you direct love toward them.

Now we will step it up a level. Picture other people you like, but do not necessarily love. A colleague, neighbor or acquaintance, for example. Imagine some of these people. Picture them in front of you, put a golden aura around them and say: *I love you* while you direct love toward them.

Then zoom out. Imagine your city or town from a bird's eye view, as if you were sitting in a helicopter looking down. Imagine the people, put a golden aura around them and say to yourself: *I love you* while directing love toward them. Then do the same with a mental image of the whole world.

Finally, the most important part. Imagine a picture of yourself. Add a gentle smile to your mental picture of yourself. Apply a golden aura. Say to yourself: *I love you!* Send strong waves of love toward yourself as you say it. Repeat this a few times. Picture yourself, add an aura and say *I love you* as you send waves of love toward yourself.

You may well be shaking your head and laughing as you read this. You might think this technique is madness. Never mind! You want to get rid of a horrendous illness and you need whatever you can get from these techniques to succeed. Do the exercise even if you think it is stupid and embarrassing. No one can see into your head, so you might as well give the technique a go, even if you think it is pointless. You have nothing to lose by giving it a try.

TECHNIQUE: LOVE MEDITATION

- Lie on a bed or soft surface, and make sure you are not going to be disturbed while you meditate.
- Start with a complete Body Scan.
- Picture someone you love on your inner mental cinema screen.
- Apply a golden aura around them.
- As you send waves of love toward them, say: *I love you.*
- Repeat with several other people (and animals). Include both people you are fond of and people you just have a superficial relationship with.
- Do the same with the city or town you live in.
- Do the same with the whole world.
- Finally, do the same with yourself.

If the Love Meditation is too intense for you, use the following alternative, a simple technique I learned from the author Tim Ferriss:

Every day, choose three people; it could be strangers or people you know. Perhaps the easiest thing could be to choose three people you meet in your day. When you meet these people, think to yourself: *I wish you a great day today.* Send a wave of good intentions to these three people and try to feel, with intensity, that you really want them to have a great day.

An additional way to increase the compassion, and eventually love, you direct toward yourself is to use a variant of the gratitude exercise you learned in Step 7. Whereas the gratitude journal involves writing down three things you appreciate and feel thankful for, this variant involves writing down things you did well today.

To do this exercise, find a notebook or something else to write on (paper-based or digital). At the end of every day, write down three things you did well today. It could be small things, like the fact that you went for a walk, or big things, such as you were able to confront some of your biggest fears. When you start out doing this exercise, it makes sense to start small. Put the bar as low as possible, so that everything you do can count as something done well. In the beginning, this exercise may feel awkward. The demon of depression might try to tell you that you didn't succeed at anything today, but that is just another of its lies. If you need to, use the Extended ABC technique from Step 10 to strip away erroneous thoughts like that, to see with a clear eye that you really DO accomplish good things in your life every day – even if you have to count rather small things in the beginning.

Using this exercise over time is a powerful way to increase your sense of self-worth and self-confidence. Over time you will notice that you automatically give yourself a metaphorical pat on the back for every single accomplishment you succeed at – big and small. And this is an important step toward appreciating yourself more, and eventually loving yourself. I have faith in you – and you will find that faith yourself!

CHAPTER SUMMARY

- At the core of most depression we find filters that color everything black and gloomy –you look at yourself, your surroundings and the world with negative eyes.

- As part of this filtering, you are likely to look at yourself with contempt, perhaps even hatred.

- To get rid of your depression, you need to get rid of these filters. The antidote to self-contempt and self-hatred is love, because love and acceptance are the antidotes to hatred and contempt.

- You can use the Love Meditation to increase the acceptance, respect, and love you feel for yourself and others.

- Alternatively, you can simply wish for three people you meet to have a great day.

- A third alternative is to write down three things every evening that you did well today.

TASKS THIS WEEK

- ☐ Take dietary supplements and eat at least a handful of vegetables every day.

- ☐ Go for a walk every day, or do some other form of aerobic exercise or movement that increases your heart rate.

- ☐ Keep a gratitude journal and add to it every evening.

- ☐ Meditate every night by performing the Love Meditation. Alternatively you can, in your head, wish three people a good day, or write down three things you did well today. Do this daily.

FURTHER READING

Kamal Ravikant: *Love Yourself Like Your Life Depends on It*

THE WEEKLY PROGRAM

To give you a better overview of the entire 14-step program, I have summarized it all here. The intention is for you to focus specifically on one topic per week, while continuing with the most important parts from the previous steps. Tick the box for each item you complete during the week. If you haven't already, sign up for the email reminders you find at kristianhall.com/system.

If you find the program below too extensive, you can make your own selection by removing items that you cannot do or that do not work for you. Alternatively, you can extend each week to be two weeks or even a month, and let the program run for a longer period.

It is essential that you *never give up on yourself*, even if you do not achieve everything in the program for one or more weeks. What is important is that you do *something*. Doing something is infinitely better than doing nothing. If you have to drop or skip a week or so, it does not matter. Simply get back on the program when you feel ready.

Whilst gradually getting rid of the habit of beating yourself up internally, you can phase in a habit of giving yourself a pat on the back every time you do something to work on your progress, and every time you do one of the techniques or follow the steps in the book. It is important to celebrate progress, no matter how small it may seem.

As you can see, I suggest you eat a *little* healthier and go for a walk every day. As I see it, these two measures are the least demanding, and the easiest to put into practice. You've come a long way if you manage to do these two things almost every day, or at least a few times during the week.

WEEK 1

- Perform a start-up ritual. It does not have to be big and complicated. You can select the short version in Step 1.
- Write in your journal about the fact that you have decided to do what you can to improve your life.

WEEK 2

- Consult your doctor to find out if you have a deficiency of vitamin D or other nutrients.
- Buy a dietary supplement containing the recommended dose (see page 62) of Omega-3, such as cod liver oil. If your doctor finds a lack of other nutrients, buy additional dietary supplements as per your doctor's recommendations.
- Take the supplements every day.
- Eat at least a handful of vegetables every day.

WEEK 3

- Take dietary supplements and eat at least a handful of vegetables every day.

- Slowly start with (more) exercise. It does not have to be more than a short walk every day. Preferably in daylight, preferably in nature, and preferably in the company of people you like and who have a positive impact on you.

WEEK 4

- Take dietary supplements and eat at least a handful of vegetables every day.
- Go for a walk every day, or do some other form of aerobic exercise or movement that increases your heart rate.
- Do the Practice with a Piece of White Paper (page 78).
- Sing or dance a little every day, or do something else that gives you positive feelings.
- Listen to uplifting music. You can find playlist suggestions at kristianhall.com.

WEEK 5

- Take dietary supplements and eat at least a handful of vegetables every day.
- Go for a walk every day, or do some other form of aerobic exercise or movement that increases your heart rate.
- Keep a sleep log. Start to become aware of how your sleep is affected by the different factors in your life. Avoid screen time before you go to bed.

WEEK 6

- Take dietary supplements and eat at least a handful of vegetables every day.
- Go for a walk every day, or do some other form of aerobic exercise or movement that increases your heart rate.

- Keep a sleep log.
- If you are not already in therapy, and have never been before, contact your doctor to start the process of finding a therapist.
- Write every day, in a journal or something similar, about how you are feeling.

Week 7

- Take dietary supplements and eat at least a handful of vegetables every day.
- Go for a walk every day, or do some other form of aerobic exercise or movement that increases your heart rate.
- Keep a gratitude journal and add to it every evening.

Week 8

- Take dietary supplements and eat at least a handful of vegetables every day.
- Go for a walk every day, or do some other form of aerobic exercise or movement that increases your heart rate.
- Keep a gratitude journal and add to it every evening.
- Try to do something enjoyable a couple of days, or evenings, during the week with people who lift you up and that you like spending time with. If you currently do not have such people around you, try to identify places you can find people like this in the future.

Week 9

- Take dietary supplements and eat at least a handful of vegetables every day.

- Go for a walk every day, or do some other form of aerobic exercise or movement that increases your heart rate.
- Keep a gratitude journal and add to it every evening.
- Do the Practice with a Piece of White Paper again.
- Reflect on what positive and negative triggers are for you, and what you can do to avoid the negative ones and get more of the positive ones (read about triggers in Step 9).

WEEK 10

- Take dietary supplements and eat at least a handful of vegetables every day.
- Go for a walk every day, or do some other form of aerobic exercise or movement that increases your heart rate.
- Keep a gratitude journal and add to it every evening.
- Practice the *Extended* ABC every day (page 146).

WEEK 11

- Take dietary supplements and eat at least a handful of vegetables every day.
- Go for a walk every day, or do some other form of aerobic exercise or movement that increases your heart rate.
- Keep a gratitude journal and add to it every evening.
- Find something you can work with to give you a greater degree of meaning in your life. Plan what you want to do with this.

WEEK 12

- Take dietary supplements and eat at least a handful of vegetables every day.

- Go for a walk every day, or do some other form of aerobic exercise or movement that increases your heart rate.
- Keep a gratitude journal and add to it every evening.
- Choose one problem in your life and make a plan to resolve it using the method in Step 12.
- Take the test on viacharacter.org.
- Plan ways to increase the sense of achievement in your life.

WEEK 13

- Take dietary supplements and eat at least a handful of vegetables every day.
- Go for a walk every day, or do some other form of aerobic exercise or movement that increases your heart rate.
- Keep a gratitude journal and add to it every evening.
- Meditate every evening by doing Body Scans (page 190). Alternative: Listen to the self-hypnosis recording every evening.

WEEK 14

- Take dietary supplements and eat at least a handful of vegetables every day.
- Go for a walk every day, or do some other form of aerobic exercise or movement that increases your heart rate.
- Keep a gratitude journal and add to it every evening.
- Meditate every night by performing the Love Meditation. Alternatively you can, within yourself, wish three people a good day. Do this daily.

When you have finished the program, continue the activities that worked best for you. You can create your own weekly program in which you give yourself weekly tasks, and then tick off each task you have completed.

Find out which activities and exercises are right for you, and make them a habit for life. This way you can prevent future relapses into depression and build a life with much greater joy and contentment.

THE WAY FORWARD

We've gone through quite a lot in this book. At the same time, the book is quite short. I have written it with the aim of it being easy to read.

I strongly encourage you to pick up some of the books in Appendix C so you get other angles of the same topics and techniques as well. The way I see it, reading about the same thing in different books and sources and then extracting the essence and key information from these different sources is an effective way to learn something new.

I have heard from many readers of *Rise from Darkness* that they have read the book several times. This can also be a good strategy for the one you are currently holding in your hands. You can read the entire book once and then go back and follow the program step by step. The book is small enough for you to carry in your bag or backpack.

If you find it difficult to work with your illness on your own, you may want to find a group of like-minded people through self-help groups. You can also ask a family member, or friend, to follow up with you during your work and help you with motivation when you find it tough.

Also, follow me on kristianhall.com, and my Facebook page fb.com/authorkristianhall, where I post instructional videos, blog posts and other tools that will help you on your journey toward a better life.

If you'd like to make me exceptionally happy, please leave me a rating or a review where you purchased the book, or on goodreads.com. This means much more to me than you can imagine!

Good luck! I wish you all the best in life.

Kristian Hall

Thank You

I t has been said that a book is always a group effort, even when it has only one author listed on the cover of the book. This has definitely been the case with this book.

I've actually had two editors working on this book. First, I worked with Jørgen Moltubak on a freelance basis. A big thank you to Jørgen for good contributions to the script.

Once I signed an agreement with my Norwegian publisher, Lise Galaasen became the editor-in-chief of the book. It is been a pleasure working with you, Lise. The quality of your input has been outstanding, and the book has turned out so much better thanks to your efforts.

In addition to the editors, I have had several proof-readers, both laymen and professionals. A big thank you to Mari, Alette, Vibeke, Cecilie, Liv-Marie, Hege, Tonje, Else Marie and Kjersti Beate. You have given me invaluable input from the perspectives of people who has either had or have depression. Thanks to this input I have been able to write and adjust the text so that it can have the best effect for the people I want to reach.

Thanks to Anne, who I worked with on my previous book, and who also provided feedback on this one.

Two professionals have reviewed the book. Knut-Petter Sætre Langlo is a psychology specialist; he assisted with the quality assurance of the academic content of the book, and also wrote the preface. Thank you very much for this very important work, Knut-Petter. My cousin Elsebeth, who is a psychiatrist, provided important input on the subject, and helped me avoid academic errors and inaccuracies. A big thank you to you, Elsebeth!

A huge thanks to my translator Christine Nicholson! You really came in as a savior for this project! Thanks also to Johanna for editing the book, Felicity for doing the proofreading and Ljiljana who designed the interior of the book.

Thank you to my mom and my sister Henriette for never giving up on me when I was unwell and making me seek therapy during my studies. This has been crucial to my own healing. In addition, I want to extend a special thank you to Henriette, who is the most energetic member of my fan club, and who helped a lot in making my first book available to the public. I can always call you for extra motivation, Henriette, and that is very important to me!

Thank you to my son, Falk, for being such a source of joy in my life. You are most precious to me. Thank you to my beautiful wife Kirsten; for who you are and for everything we have together. And a special thank you for standing by me during the years when I was still fighting my illness. Thank you for excellent and helpful input to the book as well, making it more accessible to the reader.

Many thanks to my friends for everything you give me! You know who you are. A special thank you to Harald for all the good book talks we have had.

Last but not least, thank you to all of you who have read this book. I really mean it when I say that I have written it for you. Nothing is more meaningful to me than being able to help others struggling with the troublesome illness that depression is. Never give up – just keep going until you reach a better situation in life!

I highly appreciate feedback, even when it is critical. So please send me a few words via the contact form on kristianhall.com, or via my Facebook author page. If you want to make me extra happy, write a few words about what you think of the book where you purchased it, or on goodreads.com.

Appendix A:
GLOSSARY

Adrenaline – a stress hormone that is released in, amongst others, frightening situations.

Dopamine – an important neurotransmitter that is linked to, amongst other things, the brain's reward system.

Hormone – a chemical that allows different parts of the body to communicate with each other by carrying information via various body fluids (such as blood and lymph fluid).

Meditation – mental techniques to get the brain into a different state of mind.

Neural connection – nerve cells bound together in synapses.

Neurotransmitter – a chemical that is released at a synapse, transmitting the signal from one neuron to another (or a muscle or glandular cell).

Neuron – a nerve cell.

Receptor – a substance that sits at the end of a nerve cell, receiving the neurotransmitter and then forwarding a signal. A receptor is, metaphorically, the keyhole while the neurotransmitter is the key.

Self-hypnosis–- a process of reprogramming the brain and the subconscious mind by listening to a specifically written recording repeatedly over time.

Serotonin – an important neurotransmitter between nerve cells. Low levels of serotonin may be associated with depression.

Signal substances – hormones and neurotransmitters.

Synapse – the contact area between two nerve cells, where signals can be transmitted from one nerve cell to another.

Appendix B:
List of Thought Fallacies

S ee Step 10 for a more in-depth explanation of thought fallacies (page 140).

Avoiding Responsibility	Putting the blame on other people or circumstances when you actually have a share of the responsibility.
Should-ing	Feeling guilty for not doing something you think you should do.
Filtering	Seeing only the negative aspects of a situation or an event and forgetting the positive or neutral aspects.
Generalization	Oversimplifying the world and thinking that all individuals in a certain category have the same characteristics.
Catastrophizing	Exaggerating the severity of something that happens to you, to make a disaster of a trifle or a relatively harmless incident.
Personalization	Taking for granted that events and statements are about you, even in cases where they objectively aren't.
Polarization	Dividing the world into black and white rather than the way it actually appears – in an infinitely variable scale of grey shades.
Mind-reading	Thinking that you know what others think about you, about other people or about something else, when you can't.

Appendix C:

FURTHER READING
AND RESOURCES

welcome you to my blog at kristianhall.com, where you will find plenty of posts about different ways to improve your life. Here you will also find useful resources, such as instructions for cognitive behavioral therapy techniques, as well as self-hypnosis recordings to help with insomnia, anxiety and depression. You will also find a series of instructional videos that you can use to learn various techniques.

I would also like to recommend you to sign up for my electronic newsletter, where you will receive emails with new blog posts and tips for overcoming depression. You will find the sign-up form here: http://eepurl.com/bL1nsb

BOOKS

Throughout this book I have referred to relevant further reading. There are several other books that do not necessarily fit in to a specific chapter and that are still important and good reading for anyone with depression.

Akhtar, M. (2012). *Positive Psychology for Overcoming Depression.* Watkins Publishing.

Carnegie, D. (2018). *How to Win Friends and Influence People.* Digital Fire.

Carson, R. (2003). *Taming Your Gremlin.* William Morrow Paperbacks.

Covey, S. (2004). *The 7 Habits of Highly Effective People.* Free Press.

Csikszentmihalyi, M. (1990). *Flow.* Harper Perennial.

Dispenza, J. (2007). *Evolve Your Brain.* Health Communications.

Dispenza, J. (2012). *Breaking the Habit of Being Yourself.* Hay House.

Eason, A. (2005). *The Secrets of Self-Hypnosis: Harnessing the Power of Your Unconscious Mind.* Network 3000 Publishing.

Edelman, S. (2007). *Change Your Thinking.* Marlowe & Co.

Frankl, V. E. (2013). *Man's Search for Meaning.* Ebury Digital.

Hall, K. (2015). *Rise from Darkness.* Fakkel Forlag.

Hauri, P. and Linde, S. (1996). *No more sleepless nights.* John Wiley & Sons.

Ilardi, S. (2009). *The Depression Cure: The Six-Step Program to Beat Depression Without Drugs.* Da Capo Lifelong Books.

Jeffers, S. (2007). *Feel the Fear and Do it Anyway.* Jeffers Press.

Kabat-Zinn, J. (2013). *Full Catastrophe Living.* Bantam.

Korb, A. (2015). *The Upward Spiral: Using Neuroscience to Reverse the Course of Depression, One Small Change at a Time.* New Harbinger Publications.

Leahy, R. (2006). *The Worry Cure.* Harmony.

Rankin, L. (2020). *Mind Over Medicine. Scientific Proof That You Can Heal Yourself.* Hay House UK.

Ravikant, K. (2012). *Love Yourself Like Your Life Depends on It.* Createspace.

Reivich, K. and Shatté, A. (2003). *The Resilience Factor.* Harmony.

Seligman, M. E. P. (2011). *Flourish.* Free Press.

Tolle, E. (2010). *The Power of Now.* New World Library.

Yalom, I.D. (2013). *The Gift of Therapy: An Open Letter to a New Generation of Therapists and Their Patients.* Harper Perennial.

Appendix D:
SLEEP LOG

	Date /	Date /	Date /	Date /	Date /	Date /	Date /
The time I fell asleep (approximately – do not look at the clock while trying to go to sleep)							
Approximate number of times I woke up during the night							
The time I got up							
Approximately how many hours of sleep I got last night							
The quality of my sleep last night, on a scale of 1-5 (where 5 is the best)							
Number of cups of coffee, tea and soft drinks/energy drinks I had the day before							
The time I drank the last serve of the drinks above							
Number of serves of alcohol I had the day before							
The time I drank the last serve of alcohol							
Number of cigarettes and other units of tobacco							
The time of my last cigarette and other units of tobacco							
How stressed I was the night before, on a scale of 1 to 5 (where 5 is the most stressed)							

Other factors that might have affected my sleep this week

_____

_____

_____

_____

_____

_____

_____

_____

_____

_____

_____

_____

_____

_____

_____

_____

Appendix E:

Form for Extended ABC

The Situation	Describe the situation
	What happened?
	What was the trigger(s)?
	What were you thinking?
	What feelings did you experience?
	In what other situations do you experience the same reaction?
Beliefs and thought fallacies	Which beliefs and thought fallacies are behind it?
	What is it you believe about yourself and others that led to this reaction?
	Which thought fallacies were involved?
	Are there any objective factors that support the reaction?
	Are there any objective factors that go against the reaction?
Alternative ways of thinking	How can you think about this situation in a more useful way?
	Go through the thought fallacies one by one and see what different thoughts you could have had.
	What reaction would have been more beneficial in this situation?

Printed in Great Britain
by Amazon

56563902R00147